I Wrote the Book On It

Be the Author*ity
Unlock Your Story

by Doug Crowe

I Wrote the Book On It

Copyright © 2012 by Doug Crowe

13-digit ISBN: 9781477643723
10-digit ISBN: 1477643729

Printed in USA by
Bexsi, LLC
www.authoryourbrand.com

1-800-708-2757

Dedication & Thanks

$\mathcal{J}$ dedicate this book to my parents, who imprinted upon me my self-worth and belief that life is supposed to be an abundant journey of discovery, joy and selfless service.

I also want to thank my mentors, Gary Goldstein, Darcie Newton and Kent Emmons, who showed me what it means to have integrity regardless of the dips in this journey we call life.

My drive to explore, serve and relish life is fueled by my children, Emily, Jack and Lauren who gave me the honor of being a catalyst in their success. The lessons we have taught each other are priceless. I also am blessed to have their mom, Mary, with which to share this ongoing journey. Her abundance of patience, forgiveness and faith is a necessary lesson for all writers to embrace.

Finally, I dedicate this to you. I may have not yet met you, yet, but your influence will undoubtedly touch other and for that I am grateful and blessed. May the pages you hold in your hand (paper or digital!) give you the power, insight, and road-map to thrust your story onto the stage of life for all to share.

Your story also must be told.

Tell it.

Table of Contents

Preface

You know the exact moment it happened.

It might have been in your office, at a conference or during a recent talk you gave. It doesn't matter. The fact is, someone asked you about your book. "Hey, that was a great talk. Do you have a book?" You look down at your feet, mumbled something that sounded witty and deflect the obvious.

You don't have a book.

You've thought about writing one. You have a compelling story. Your business has a unique spin. Your mom said you are brilliant. A client asked you to write one. The story is the same across any industry.

You have a book inside you and you know it.

The benefits of being an author have done wonders for your competition. Moreover, your mentor, coach, and even "A" list national figures whom you admire, all have a book or two in the marketplace. You may have even used some of their material to build your brand or business.

But you are different. Your strategy, ideas and story is as unique as you. You've had some great ideas and have a unique story to tell. If only it could be in print for all to see and share.

It is a stone-cold fact that the professional who has a published book is ALWAYS perceived as an expert in their industry. Even some celebrities who can perceived as shallow or self-serving tend to be held in higher regard once they have a book published.

Why?

The reason *published* authors have MORE credibility, MORE clients, MORE recognition and MORE income is because the human race traditionally learns from books. The authors of books are revered. The authors of books are credible experts. We have been trained from birth to learn from an authority figure and the most respected teachers from Aristotle, Shakespeare and your high school English composition teacher all had the gift of educating through the written word. A tremendous amount of your education has come from books. Sure, you have learned a great deal from experience, but books and the authors who create them are always behind every lesson. There are a myriad of reasons the credible expert in any industry continues to be recognized as the authority. The biggest reason is obvious.

It's not easy to get a book done!

It takes a tremendous amount of skill, patience, time and money to create and publish a book. Even with hundreds of self-publishing websites and assitance, it is this Hurculean effort that is still recognized to this day as a significant milestone in anyone's career.

How about you?

What will it mean to you to take your 'status' as the local or regional "go-to" person to a *nationally* known brand? More importantly, with a book as your foundation what will your business look like with a <u>suite</u> (the book is only the first) of high-margin products delivering cash into your bank account while you are sleeping?

With a book, your message, marketing and sales will be working not only 24/7 but 24/7 to the 10,000 power. Your book will be a silent sales person, repeating your message and your content to untold thousands or even millions of people. Your new tribe will become loyal, raving fans that would be clamoring to become part of your sphere of influence. A book doesn't ask for days off. A book doesn't require workmen's compensation and a book doesn't sleep. A book is relentless. YOUR book is as close to cloning as you can get. Your book will do for you what no staff, advertising or marketing system can come close to.

It will make you a national authority and pay you royalties for decades. It will transform any outbound marketing efforts to inbound inquiries. Your book can become an automated education-based marketing and sales system for your current business and become a launching pad for other information-based products you haven't even created yet.

Do you realize how much freedom, money and peace you will enjoy being a published author? Do you realize how good it will FEEL to have people asking you to sign your book? (Get over any modesty you may harbor…the recognition is earned)

The book you hold in your hands, however isn't really a book about you. We don't have the depth and details about your brand, company or story-yet. This is not a 200-page, lengthy, exploration of the publishing industry. Nor is it intended to take more than an hour or so to digest. The meat of this book will give you a blueprint for success on the journey to becoming a published author.

It comes as no surprise, of course, that our firm has three distinct areas where we can help you with this process.

Do It Yourself. You can read this book, subscribe to our newsletter, use the blueprint and get your book created, published and marketed. There are no "secrets" to this process… only hard work, timeless persistence, the patience to follow the plan and the financial resources to pull it off.

Classroom & Mentorship. Nobody writes their own book. Everyone graduates as a published author! The online classes take a handful of authors through the entire process of positioning, creation, publishing, marketing and promotion. The classes include all of the materials, tools and personal interaction to get your book written and your business booming. Each week, a milestone (homework) automatically creates each component of your book, brand and launch. Enrollment is limited.

We Do it All. This option, of course, saves you the most time and eliminates the pricey mistakes that you *will* make when you attempt this rather complicated task alone. The financial requirements are higher. The pay-off is that your book will be done in about 100 days. If you qualify for our publishing option, your book will be marketed very effectively.

This introductory book is designed to be read quickly and implemented steadily. It was written to give you a glimpse at the details and provide anyone with a clear blueprint on launching your brand.

If you take this path of doing it yourself, do yourself a huge favor. Don't just read it. What a shame it would be if you simply read it, nodded your head and "played" with a few of the ideas. If you plan on writing and marketing your own book, you will have to budget a consistent amount of time and resources to finishing.

How much time?

That depends on the method you use to write. Some people write on a computer. Others dictate and have it transcribed. Others may simply take their articles, notes and interviews and hire a ghost writer. Extremely busy professionals are interviewed by a journalist and outsource all the various tasks to other professionals. Any of these methods work. The path you take will determine the amount of money and time invested.

Consider how your business will transform when your marketing costs drop through the floor and people start calling

YOU for interviews, speaking opportunities and sales. Imagine how your business will explode with a host of other products and services that you can deliver quickly, easily and with tremendous margins. Imagine what it will feel like to a have a full schedule of hungry clients, who you don't have to sell, influence or market to. Get ready to transform your outbound "push" strategy to an inbound "pull" strategy of having prospects contacting you or your office and becoming clients faster than ever before.

Take a moment on your next sleepless night, layover or traffic jam to consider how your life will dramatically improve once you have a book published about you, your brand and your company.

Let's create your book.

Introduction

I know you.

You are one of those positive, encouraging, entrepreneur types. You always look on the bright side of life, your attitude is up, you like upbeat music and you are the quite often the life of the party. Your greatest asset is that people like you and you're are at the top of your game. Your business has such massive potential. You even plan for future expansion in the midst of your competitors laying people off. Right?

No?

It doesn't matter if you have a positive, growth-oriented attitude or if you are hunkering down to weather the storm of the most recent economic slide. Your business is either growing or dying and you know it. It is up to YOU to take the bull by the horns, make tough decisions to serve your clients, company and your family. While it is acceptable to be mindful of the local and national economic macro trends, it is unacceptable to engage in any excuses. Excuses don't solve challenges.

As you fly through the pages in this book, you may have a tendency to gloss over and skim it. Hey, I get it. You are busy! I have made matters worse by eliminating the normal 30 pages of examples and stories to support the point necessary in each chapter.

That's a good thing.

I know you have limited time to read (and even LESS time to sit down and write a book!) Fortunately, if you do skim it, you should remember the points in each chapter and this will make it easy to refer back to once you begin your journey to create the market-shifting strategy of becoming an author. If you enjoy the long examples and supportive stories of other books, please refer to the references located at the end of this one. There are over a dozen titles that you can refer to and use with great success. This book is designed to be read and used...*quickly*.

NOTE: 99% of the people will not take the time to create and publish their book.
Go DIRECTLY to the last chapter
and learn about your options for ACTION.
www.authoryourbrand.com

The resources, ideas and concepts have been distilled down into bite-sized chunks so that in less than an hour or two, you will have all the ammunition you need to start creating your book. If you USE the concepts, resources and advice in this book, your book can be completed quickly and you can begin to shift your business from the struggles many entrepreneurs have to the peace and abundance that so few have.

With an integrated marketing campaign and consistent effort you can even be a best selling author within a year! Imagine what the title, "Best Selling Author" on your by-line or website will do for your credibility, status and business clout.

{Your Name}: Best Selling Author.

Chapter 1

Why You Must Have a Book

*Y*our clients love you-right?

Over the years you have served them well and the top percentage probably think you walk on water. There are others who appreciate you and simply view you as the obvious choice for what you do. These people have, through buying your services, provided for your family, allowed you to build a business and a lifestyle that you have created.

What about your competitors' clients?

What do they say about you? Do they even know you exist? The clients you *don't* have are buying from and following your competitors. Your mission is to not acquire new clients and increase revenue. Your mission is to **overwhelm** the landscape with your status as the "go to" person in your defined niche. How do you do that? Simply stated, there are only a few ways to increase revenue. As Jay Abraham notes in his book, "Getting Everything You Can Out of All You Got" there are only a few areas where increase revenue can come from.

- Increase the number of clients
- Increase the number of referrals from clients
- Increase the number of products/services
- Decrease the cost of goods/services you provide

This book will give you clear strategies to hit all of these areas SIMULTANEOUSLY. No other marketing strategy, tactic or sales course can claim that. Only a professionally packaged and marketed book about you and your brand can take you from obscurity to fame in a matter of months. Only a book about you and your unique message will attract new clients, give you more referrals, add new product lines and decrease your marketing costs…all in one move.

Brilliant.

Most professionals and entrepreneurs want to increase their business, decrease their overhead and move from the 80-hour workweek to the 30-hour or 20-hour workweek and enjoy MORE income.

What will it take the accomplish that? There is only one path to more income and less time.

Royalty-based income.

If you are already on track to do that-great. A book will accelerate and solidify your position. If, however, you are like most business owners and professionals, you may be taking more time to earn the same revenue as a few years ago. In fact, many of the doctors, sales reps and business owners I have spoken to have lamented that it is taking MORE dollars and time to acquire FEWER customers than ever before.

Regardless of your situation, a book about you and your brand can do for you what no other marketing brochure, web 2.0 strategy or stand alone Facebook campaign can even come close to.

Your book can make you the authority in your field.

What will it feel like to increase your business by 20, 30 or even a 100% over the course of the year? What would it mean to your business if you could shift your marketing from the outbound "Notice Me!" syndrome of flyers, email, social media, referrals, chamber events, trade shows, telemarketing, sales force, etc. to a strategy where your fans/clients/customers simply call you and ask when they can start to hand over their cash?

You need a book about you and your company.

The reasons are there. You see it every time you turn on FOX News, CNN, Larry King or listen to an author on the radio. Experts get the interviews. Authors are perceived as the experts.

What about you?

You know in your gut that your experience and knowledge

is equal to or greater than the speaker at your last trade show. That individual probably invested serious resources into developing his/her content, packaging it into a book and promoting it in an intelligent and effective manner.

Take a moment and reflect upon the top 2-3 people in your industry. I don't mean locally. Think about the top people in your industry. In the notes section in this chapter write down the top 3 books in your profession and note the most well known professionals whom you read about, admire or respect.

Don't filter out personality or experience, either. If you are a doctor and don't care for Dr. Oz or Dr. Phil, put your professional opinion aside. Your mission is not to put them down because they don't share your values or experience. Your job is to find out all the details about their business and the fantastic reach they have achieved as professional *business* owners, not doctors.

If you're a sales professional, remember that Zig Ziglar and Brian Tracy started out exactly where you are today. They sold stuff and then they taught others "how they did it." Can you guess which path created more freedom, lifestyle and peace of mind? You don't have to want to be a public speaker or marketing guru in order to earn a high six or seven figure passive income. But you do have to have a book.

A book will give you status.

Your book can make you a sought after interviewee.

You will become an authority figure who gets the call from your local newspaper and radio station to comment on your profession. Curiously, your book will end up being purchased by your competitors as well!

Some businesses operate in a scarcity mode. There are only so many clients out there and you work relentlessly to serve the ones you have and attract new ones away from your competitors. This can be a geographic stumbling block or simply a niche issue.

But authors have none of these restrictions.

It is ridiculous to think you can have ALL of the clients in any particular industry, of course. Our free market society has all but eliminated monopolies. It doesn't matter if you are the only game in town because even customer apathy is a competitive thorn in the sides of many business owners.

As the economy ebbs and flows, consumers and B2B clients adjust their buying habits and attitudes. What was once a necessity becomes a luxury. In order to compete, survive and thrive, you need to work smarter, not harder. Since it is impossible to create more time for yourself, consider the strategy that has worked consistently during recessions, depressions and technological revolutions.

Become an expert author. Become the authority.

Your business and brand can be bigger than it is today. No matter where you are in your personal business cycle, satellite offices, employee growth and 9 figure revenue goals have popped in your head at one time or anther. Perhaps they are still there. A book can carry you there faster than conventional (and expensive) traditional marketing.

We'll show you how to use your book to overcome the scarcity mindset of your competitors, and in one samurai move, turn your competition into your partners, your clients into raving fans and your bottom line solidly into the black.

Co-opetition

No…it's not a misprint. Competition meets cooperation. The phrase may or may not be new to you, but co-opetition is the way to transform a relationship with your former competitors, not ignore, tolerate or try to outsmart them.

Once again, your book and expert status can achieve a multitude of positive results in a single move. When you have a book that specifically delivers fresh, relevant and useful content for your clients, your competition will use it. You are already doing the same!

The last time you read an article and embedded it into your sales literature, you essentially took information and positioned it to benefit your company. Companies, individuals and professionals do this on all the time as they increase their knowledge and competitive advantage. Maybe you picked up a sales tactic from superstar Chet Holmes. If you are a doctor, you may have used a new study from the New England Journal of Medicine to better serve your patients. Regardless of the source, you increased your knowledge from the efforts, education and mistakes of others.

What if YOU were that source?

98% of the sources you use today for your business are never quoted, referenced or even known by your clients. But when you publish your book, you put your name right alongside a phrase, concept or strategy that, by copyright, you claim as your own. You have now drawn a line in the sand and created a reference that 98% of your readers, like you, won't give you credit for! What? No citation? No foot-note?

It's possible. However, if you were to seek out these readers with intent, you can change the connection to you significantly. Instead of the thousands of people who "borrow" your content and intellectual property without regard to referencing your brilliance, you can have hundreds not only referenced your name as the source, but you actually **pay you** to spread your own words!

Here's how it works:

1. Hire a team to create your book.

2. Design an integrative campaign to use your authoritative status with your business.

3. Market your message with speaking gigs, online, offline and a hundred other ways referenced in this book and the sources listed in our resource guide.

4. Contact your competition and offer them referral fees, commission and joint venture agreements.

You are an authority. Being a published author places you in a position of power and makes you the expert. You have other people in your field that YOU look up to…why not BE one of them! Turn the tables in your head. What would it mean to you if Tony Hsieh, CEO of Zappos asked YOU to promote his book WITH him, not for him? Would you do it? Of course! Any alignment or association with a public figure, by its very nature, elevates your status.

The good news is you don't have to wait to become a billion dollar company to start. A few years ago, Gary Vaynerchuk was a local wine seller. Because he wrote and published a book, he has become a marketing maven. (www.crushitbook.com) Every millionaire expert and authority begins by being successful and making their mark in business. Once they have achieved some significance, the FIRST step is to create that book about their journey, mission or differentiating factor. We all love a good story and YOUR story must be told and shared with your clients, prospects and even your competition.

Become the authority. Start your journey right now and reap the rewards that have proven to be the game changer for thousands of business owners and professionals worldwide.

Some entrepreneurs I have spoken to lament the fact that they don't feel they have anything new or unique to say. Further, they may feel that being a new business prevents them from being perceived as the expert.

Hogwash.

There are two distinct paths authors take:

1. Your story, experience and success is interesting to others.

2. Research and compile the success of others and package it.

Either path has proven to shower the author with eternal notoriety, status and success. You don't have to have 20 years of experience or a life-threatening story to share to be successful as an author. That is one path and if you have it-use it.

Hundreds of business owners and professionals are reaping the rewards of being published authors and cashing in on their status as experts. Many of them have not only increased their income with a book, many have exceeded their professional income using their book as a platform for incremental revenue that literally transforms their life.

In fact, I challenge you to find one seven-figure income earner in your field who has a boatload of time on their hands who does not have a book. This challenge comes with a prize, my dear reader. Send me the name of any seven-figure income earner in your field who does not have a book published. If they sign up for our newsletter, you will be entitled to a gift from us. If they enroll as a client with us in ANY capacity, your gift will be exceedingly generous. Simply drop me a line at doug@dougcrowe.com. There…shameless promotion meets challenge.

Take a few minutes and answer the following questions. You will move yourself closer to manifesting the physical book and results you seek.

List 3 ways your book will serve others

1. _____

2. _____

3. _____

List 3 of your favorite books and why

1. _____

2. _____

3. _____

List 3 benefits a book will create for your business

1. _____

2. _____

3. _____

Chapter 2

The Stress-Free Entrepreneur

*W*hat stresses you out? Does health care reform keep you awake at night? Does the unknown of your competitors marketing campaign create hesitation with your initiatives?

First of all, stress is the major catalyst for all health related disease and death, so my first bit of advice is to take a breath, step back and get into one of my favorite books, *How to Stop Worrying and Start Living* by Dale Carnegie.

As the owner of your own business, you are plagued with payroll, legal, employees, vendors, marketing, sales, accounting, leases, and thousands of other variables, any one of which can cause you to question your sanity.

What would happen to your stress, peace of mind and lifestyle if you had *too many* clients?

How would it feel if you had more inbound activity (people calling you asking for your products and services) as opposed to outbound activity (you marketing and promoting yourself). There is a fundamental and massive stress-reducing shift that occurs when you transform your marketing and branding in this strategic manner.

With the nuclear explosion of the web and personal media, it has become exceedingly difficult to capture your client's attention. There are over 11.5+ billion web pages to choose from, hundreds of cable channels, and we are pummeled with over 2 billion YouTube videos daily.

Do you really believe you have a unique USP (unique selling proposition)? Your ability to cut through the exponentially increasing amount of clutter is nearly impossible. The ONLY thing unique to this world and your industry is you. With over 11 billion websites, rest assured there is a competitor with more money, more experience and more clients that has an identical USP, lower prices or higher quality. The only differentiator available to you is your unique story.

Put it in a book.

How loyal are your clients? Do they stay with you regardless of the "new" thing or the coupon from your competitors? What about new clients? How do you effectively and affordably reach them and influence them to work with you?

Most business owners create a marketing plan based on what they like and what "looks" good to them. A convincing advertising representative can influence you to invest in his print, SEO or other media campaign based on how many people are "tuning in" or viewing his media.

Where does all of this lead?

Into the void of the unknown.

Multi-million dollar ad budgets are placed, executed and rolled out on a high degree of emotion, a bit of statistics and a backwards look at what has had some success in the past. Even marketing goliaths like Unilever, Coca-Cola or Proctor and Gamble have to adapt to the changing landscape.

The problem with marketing isn't simply the fact that people are bombarded with over 3,000 messages per day and forget 2,997 of them within 3 seconds of the impression. The real issue is that getting someone's attention via a "push" or "interruption marketing" becomes less effective with volume. Just as we get used to background noise in a Starbucks as we are writing (as I am now), we get used to the clutter of marketing messages as the volume, frequency and intensity increases.

The marketer's answer has traditionally been to assault our senses with an increase of volume (bigger or brighter messaging) or frequency (repetition breeds familiarity). Even being unique doesn't work anymore. As Seth Godin discusses in his book, "Purple Cow," if we see a purple cow, it gets our attention. But, after seeing more and more purple cows, they become as common as a regular cow and become uninteresting over time.

The megatrend in marketing espoused by leaders such as Chet Holmes, Seth Godin, Jay Conrad Levinson, and dozens of others is to provide rich, valuable and relevant content. The quality and frequency of your content (not advertising) is what consumer and B2B clients are searching for anyway…why pester them with an advertisement when they spend 99% of their time online looking for data.

Forget the sales pitch. Your job is to give them what they are looking for, not what you have to sell. If you do it right, you will never have to sell them. They will come to you and beg you to buy whatever you are selling after they know you, like you and trust you. (Hint: I am doing that right now for YOU!)

What does all of this have to do with stress?

Plenty.

Once you embrace the strategy of becoming the expert and orient all of your "marketing" to public relations and content provider, your clients will begin to know who you are. They will become consistently addicted to what you have to say and when the time is right, they will ask you to give them more.

Nobody likes to be sold, but everyone likes to buy.

With a shift in focus from marketing *you* and how wonderful you are towards providing relevant content to your target audience, your outbound reach to clients via a "push" strategy will become an effortless "pull" strategy. These results will have your target audience coming to you for your advice, goods and services.

Who would you rather deal with, an unknown vendor with a pretty website or a published author, who was featured in the local media as the expert on his topic?

Duh.

In the early 2000's I started a real estate training company for investors. With the proliferation of boot camps and week-end seminars, I was immersed in a sea of slick marketing and high-credit card limits. The basics of adult education in this arena were universal and I was trapped into providing similar content that everyone else was providing.

There was no way I was going to compete from a position of authenticity and service by competing head on with the likes of Robert Allen, Carleton Sheets and dozens of other "A" players in the real estate investment world. My big value and key differentiator was that the content I would deliver would not be oriented to my schedule and my desire for fast money. I would deliver it in a context that worked for the client.

We opened up an academy with a 10-week curriculum and a 6-month training course. The academy was a traditional brick and mortar enterprise that gave instant and customized feedback to the clients. We founded the nations' only semester-based, live real estate academy for real estate investors. The only way a student "graduated" was they had to invest in a property.

We held them accountable to a tangible output.

Like any business, we advertised. We placed ads through local media channels, did telemarketing and attended trade shows. We invested heavily in the marketing of our academy

---

NOTE: We use the same system for the Author Your Brand online classes where the weekly output of homework actually creates the book for the students. We provide the ONLY training in the world where a tangible product is delivered at the conclusion of the training.
www.AuthorYourBrand.com

---

and began to enroll students on a consistent basis. The stress of hunting for clients was wearing us all down. We needed a shift.

In January of 2003, I came up with the initiative to create a 180-degree shift in our marketing. I told our staff that I wanted to "fire" all the outbound sales efforts and have 100% of our efforts go to handling inquiries from our PR. I gave them a year to design, execute and manage to pull this off.

We did it in 6 months.

The stress of constantly hunting or farming for clients took a dramatic shift. We went from a monthly outlook on our sales numbers to a media focus on how many people were reading my book, attending our seminars, listening to our radio program and referring their friends. Our marketing expenses went from double-digit percentage of our revenue to single digits. We not only made over 150% more in revenue, but our marketing costs declined by over 50%!

More importantly, as the stress disappeared, our margins on our revenue increased. Our classed filled to capacity. We began enrolling students 2 and 3 semester into the future. Instead of the stress of not knowing where the next client would come from, we had a waiting list and we focused on providing great content for our community, qualifying candidates for the right fit and creating a waiting list for future enrollees.

Imagine having the ability to screen clients! Because we focused on the success of our students, we treated our academy like a real school (it wasn't chartered). Just like Author Your Brand we actually have to turn some people away who didn't pass the entrance exam!

This marketing, revenue and margin shift was a direct result of the brand we built as an expert. We had a radio show, did seminars and published a book on investing. I was an expert. Was I an expert because I had more experience? In some ways, yes. But there were plenty of other experts who had much more experience than me. What separated our academy from every other opportunity was the fact that I was a published author and radio host.

Putting your content, story and message in print establishes you as an expert. Getting on stages, speaking on the radio and being profiled in other media normally occurs BECAUSE you have a book.

When you begin with a book and put the proper marketing and PR push behind it, you can eliminate the stress of chasing prospects, accepting sub-standard credit risks or hunting for your next big deal. You can enjoy the status of being the "go to" person in the media and become the guy at the trade show who doesn't pay to have a booth, but GETS paid to speak, share and solidify his brand.

List 3 stress points in your business

1. _____

2. _____

3. _____

List 3 ways your book will reduce that stress

1. _____

2. _____

3. _____

 # Multiply Your Time & Money

"But Doug, doesn't writing a book, hiring a PR firm and attracting media attention cost a ton of money?"

Yes. It can.

Ask any author who got started without the help of a miserly consultant! Many public relations firm charge thousands of dollars per month to promote you, your brand and your book. Even those that "guarantee" placement don't guarantee sales or specific exposure. It is far easier to spend and waste money than it is to earn it. When self-made billionaire, Marvin Davis, was asked in Forbes Magazine how to make money, he said that he has one simple rule and it is, "Don't lose money." If you focus on not losing it, your investments will be wiser and more abundant.

This is tough advice for risk-taking entrepreneurs, but worth consideration when analyzing marketing strategies and tactics.

Reflect heavily upon the facts; with the exception of direct response marketing or CPA (click per action), advertising is a crapshoot. You toss your message out there on a constant basis in hopes that you will capture the attention of a ready, willing and able prospect. Throwing mud on the wall is not only a haphazard strategy, but also one that is nearly impossible to track, refine or improve upon.

As a new author, you will have humble beginnings when it comes to marketing and tracking your new brand as a published expert. Therefore, what dollars you do invest, need to have leverage.

I am a huge fan of investing in any action, message, strategy or tactic that has leverage. When I refer to leverage I am describing it not as getting a $1,000 advertisement for $200, but executing a specific strategy that has more than one measurable outcome.

For example, let's say you agree to speak at a local community college. Universities book speakers all the time and there are speakers, such as James Malinchak, who make considerable incomes focusing primarily on the college market. You agree to give a talk on leadership and your book has a theme that resonates with that title. Your booked 60 days in advance. Your fee is a modest $1,000, but you want the experience. Even assuming your book would be a good fit for your audience, college students are not the wealthiest crowd out there. You are told the audience attendance ranges from 200-400 people. You anticipate selling 50-100 books in addition to your speaking fee. That might add up to an additional few hundred dollars. Not a terrible income for working an hour or two.

Let's leverage this event.

1. Call ALL of the other universities in the area and let them know you are speaking at XYZ University. Since you are already in the area, you can honestly waive your travel expenses and offer to speak at their location.

2. Contact the local chamber of commerce and offer them the same. If they have already booked a speaker for that month's meeting, invite their members to the talk you have scheduled at the university.

3. Contact the *other* organizations at the University that would benefit from your talk and invite them as well. Don't depend on the college promoter to pack your house. Take 100% responsibility for filling every seat.

4. Contact the student paper and offer to do an interview about your upcoming talk. Better yet, let them know YOU would like to interview an interesting campus celebrity and offer the interview or article for free to the paper.

5. Contact student leadership and offer them a referral or commission for moving more tickets (if it's a paid event) or selling more of your books for you. College kids are hungry for money and anything you can do to serve THEM, the better.

6. Contact faculty and administrative leadership and invite them to do a panel discussion or other involvement with

your talk. Getting more leaders to attend makes you look good and plants the seed for future bookings of speeches, trainings and book sales.

7. Contact the campus, local and regional radio, TV, and newspapers and let them know you are speaking at the college. Align your message with the news. Without a connection to a current news story, your message probably won't get much press (more in Chapter 9).

A book can give you more leverage (and a tremendous ROI) than any other strategy, tactic or media campaign. A single placement in the newspaper ends up in a birdcage or landfill within 24 hours. Your online ad, if you are lucky, may be read by 1/10 of 1% of viewers. Broadcasting is being replaced with nanocasting and microcasting. The common element is that you are "casting!" Like tossing a line in the water and the bait slipping off, marketing via casting is a loose, imperfect and haphazard method to acquire customers. Not so with your book. Why?

People rarely discard a book.

Your book will not only give you the status of being the expert, but when intelligently positioned, it can give you tremendous leverage for speaking fees, training programs, CD sales (audio books), book sales, not to mention increasing the sales of your current product or service.

Your book is the ultimate lever where a single book signing or conversation can pay you in 4 or 5 ways many times over.

Your budget for promoting your book need not be lavish to be effective. One of the corollaries to the proliferation of media, web 2.0 and social media outlets is a reduction in cost. 10 years ago, a mortgage provider seeking 1,000 highly targeted prospects online might have paid $30 per client with an aggressive lead generation campaign. Today, you can start a Facebook fan page about mortgage deals, write a short ebook about the pitfalls of refinance and reach 1,000 highly targeted prospects for absolutely zero cost!

When investing your hard earned dollars, always consider the low budget alternative. It usually takes more time, but can often deliver longer-lasting results. For example, a CPC (cost per click) campaign on Google can give you instant results. You will need to test your copy, have decent conversions, bid on appropriate keywords and monitor the campaign hourly to insure you don't blow it. This strategy is one that has sucked more money from entrepreneurial wallets than a politician. Get professional help when running any CPC campaign. Contact us for a list of resources.

An 'organic' tactic to build an audience is to blog and post short video clips every week on YouTube and embed the proper links and keywords in your content. You can have an equal amount of traffic in a few months for zero cost. Building organic traffic is slower, but is perceived as more authentic. Paid traffic is instant, and once you refine your conversion process, it gives you a license to print money. Both strategies work. In the end, you always trade time for money.

Similarly, you can sit down and crank out a book about your brand, message and story. Many authors take months or years to craft their message, hire an editor, designer and contact an agent to represent the manuscript to publishers. The average book, once completed, takes 18 months to hit the bookshelves. That, of course, assumes that a publisher even wants to publish your work. Your chances of hitting the book stores is about as likely as winning the American Idol competition.

With the advent of self-publishing, anyone can "print" a book and even post it to Amazon or Barnes & Noble. Beware, however, without an intelligently designed position and a marketing campaign to engage an audience, like most marketing, it'll end up in the dead zone.

In order to craft a compelling message, you must NOT do what nearly ALL unsuccessful authors do and become obsessed with what successful authors do.

Think.

You have a concept. Your story has been percolating for years and you even have a few titles you like. Where do you begin? Many author's believe their story or journey are the reason people want to read their book, but that is never the case.

Nobody cares about your story.

They do care about THEIR story and how your message and ideas can help them lead a better life. Unless you are a celebrity, nobody really cares about you.

It's about them.

Stories are great. In fact, they are necessary. Your story may support, reaffirm or explain your premise. It can even be entertaining, but it should not be confused with the purpose of your book.

Your message must do more than cause a reader to think. You want to compell them to act. The first action must be to turn to the subsequent page. The term "page turner" means you've done a great job of keeping the reader engaged and creating a burning desire for them to wan to know more.

A great book will be one the reader can't put down without finishing.

How do you do this?

Dissection of the Book Buying Process

Consider what YOU do when you go by a bookshelf. Freeze a few moments in time and realize the steps you take in analyzing a book and deciding. Your first thoughts are not "should I read this or not." Your first thoughts are "should I even pick it up. "

I visit book stores, both online and offline every week. I love covers. I love the way colors are juxtaposed with words. I enjoy analyzing how images are used to grab my attention and cause me to think.

However, the ONLY reason to have a compelling cover is to get the potential reader to do one important thing…stop, touch the book and turn it over to read the back cover. That's it. It is similar to a headline in a newspaper. The ONLY function of that headline is to interrupt your current thought and get you to want to read the next line.

The purpose of the back cover is to get the reader to open the book and scan the table of contents. The table of contents is designed to get them to flip through and buy the book. Therefore, the structure of your book's title, cover and table of contents is designed 100% as an exercise in marketing and psychology.

After that process is refined (and tested with your readers) how does one **structure** the content in an engaging way?

How do you write it?

Many authors use a combination of interviews, blog posts, articles, audios or videos to compile and orgainze their message and story. You may even have some journal entries you can use. (But your book will NOT sell if it is merely a diary of your life's journey)

How do you transform this mass of content into something resembling a nonfiction book?

Developing Your Book's Theme & Framework

In order to have a book and message that is unique, compelling and flows nicely you must organize it into a compelling theme and clear framework. Your theme must be unique and, like your body's skeleton, be built upon a framework.

No theme. No interest.

No framework. No support.

Your unique message (it is unique-right?) must be presented in an easy to read manner. We'll get to the context in a moment, but before we talk about bullet points and spacing, the content needs to be organized in a unique theme that you can claim as your own.

Newsflash: Your topic has already been written about.

I'm not saying there are not any new ideas, but there is a 99.9% chance YOUR topic and even a *better* version of your story, has already been told.

Your job, as a new author, is to build a theme and framework for your message that is unique to you, compelling to your reader and easily passed on to others.

Here's an example:

You may have seen the video, read the book or heard the audio "The Secret" by Rhonda Byrne.

People spoke about "The Secret" ad nauseum. There are "Law of Attraction" parties, vision board companies and thousands of products, brands and spin off's from this book and movie.

Only it wasn't original.

If you trace "The Law of Attraction" back a generation, you'll find it solidly planted in the book, *Think and Grow Rich*, originally printed in 1937.

Only it wasn't original.

If you trace back THAT book to its roots, you'll find another book by Wallace Wattles, called, *The Science of Getting Rich*, published in 1910. Wattles took a very "New Age" concept of the universal laws of energy, thought and the universe and positioned it in a scientific manner for all to learn and apply.

This wasn't original, either.

You see, just a 8 years earlier, James Allen wrote the book, *As a Man Thinketh*. Mr. Allen spoke about the wonders of the "Law of Attraction" and how thoughts become things. He interlaced plenty of morality and character-building wisdom in his books, too.

Wait! I'm still not done. Do you realize that the sum total of nearly all of this wisdom can be found in another book, written a few thousand years earlier?

It's called the Bible.

My point (if it isn't obvious yet) is that your thoughts, message and ideas may not be new (unlikely) but that will NOT prevent you from positioning it in a unique manner.

Rhonda Byrne's "The Secret" lit off a firestorm of awareness for a timeless message that has been written, re-written and discussed for thousands of years. The only difference was the manner in which she **positioned** her message.

Do you already have a theme? Write it down now.

_____

_____

_____

_____

If you don't, don't worry. We will help you craft a unique one.

Make it easy to understand and it will be easy to share.

Framework

Your job is to take your ideas and build a unique and compelling framework that readers can easily digest.

Another framework example can be found in Stephen Covey's *The 7 Habits of Highly Effective People.*

No curiosity here. Stephen tells you EXACTLY what the book is about on the cover.

The visual representation of his framework is his double triangle graphic that shows how the 7 habits are related to each other.

After you have an overall theme for your book, create a framework that can be easily placed on a 3x5 notecard or readily shared by other people.

The reason the 7 Habits is easy to remember is not only because of the 7 things (our mind works well to remember 7 digits with a dash, hence our phone number and social security numbers are broken up with dashes), but also because of the graphical representation of the concept.

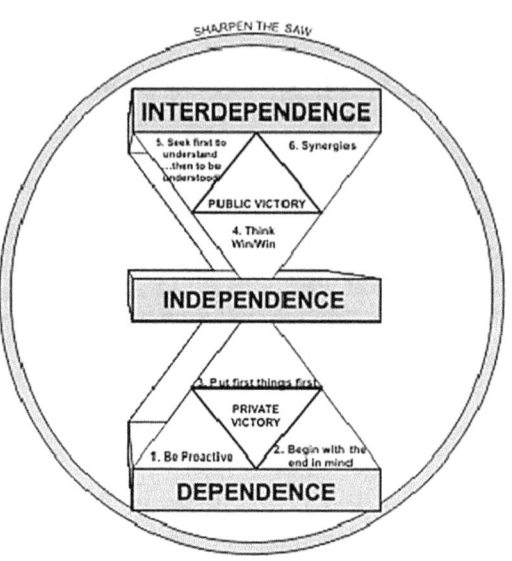

Your framework can be as simple as a single word (*Blink* or *The Secret*) or as robust as the 7 habits, but you must have one. Without a framework, your book will be a stream of consciousness that half of your readers won't retain and most won't share effectively.

Organizing Your Book's Content

Now that you have a compelling theme and a framework to build upon, its time to organize your content.

Writing is tough.

It is even tougher to write well.

The reason you will have prestige and credibility as an author is because wrting a book is difficult! The proprietary methodology we use to create your book are avoided or not even known by thousands of unsuccessful authors.

Our job is to help you become a *successful* author.

At *Author Your Brand* academy, we'll walk you through the creation, development and refinement of your theme, positioning and framing of your message.

Once we have that framework established, your job as the "author" (not the writer) is 90% done. When a judicious amount of time and energy is invested in the development of your theme, position and framework, the rest of the work is easy.

Let's get your content out of your brain and into print….intelligently. Here are a few things you can do to help the process of creating your book with our team.

Take Inventory

Take an inventory of your content.

Organize and label each piece of content you have. Review your list and bring some consistency to your topics. You may or may not have previously written articles, blogs, photos or interviews. Whatever you have take stock, categorize them and put in a spreadsheet or list by category, topic or media source.

List your topics (some may become book titles) that you know about or feel your audience wants to read about.

1.

2.

3.

4.

5.

6.

7.

8.

9.

10.

Next Step

We'll help you develop your positioning and framework, design a great book cover, title, outline and write a **great book** for you!

Title, content, design, editing, proofing, framework, etc… the list of nuances, pitfalls and important tasks is endless. With the Author Your Brand outcome-based system, you won't write a word, but your book will be compelling.

Contact us today to see how to apply for our academy. The enrollment process takes a few moments and we can answer all of your quesitons.

If accepted, your book can be on the shelves of Amazon.com in under 100 days. Give us a call today. 1-800-708-2757

Money Saving Tips

1. **Write the book yourself**. Yeah...I know, it's a pain in the rear, but taking 15-20 minutes every day and simply putting your thoughts on paper (digital, of course) in a few months, your content will be in a position to be organized. Hiring a ghostwriter or using our services will shorten your burden by a year or more, but if you have the patience or abundance of free time, go ahead and start! You will be hiring an editor, anyway, so don't feel your first draft has to be perfect. By consistently writing a bit each day, in a few months, your first draft can be completed.

2. **Hire College interns.** There are thousands of Universities that have an abundance of talented people who are majoring in journalism, English or creative writing. Consider posting an internship on a job board and getting a student to assist you in crafting your story, editing and proofing your work. www.internships.com is a good start.

3. **Virtual Assistant.** There are scores of professional marketers, authors and experts who have multi-million dollar businesses with no staff (or very little). Consider the ad-

vantages of getting an assistant to take care of your low priority tasks and tackle the jobs that don't add to your bottom line. I have several assistants that book flights, edit copy or do research that do it quicker and better than I could. NOTE: It is nearly impossible to outsource your voice…for media interviews, speaking engagements and book signings, the author and expert needs to be seen and heard. Try recruiting from outsourcing sites such as, www.elance.com, www.odesk.com, www.guru.com, www.twitter.com, www.craigslist.org or other sites listed in the resource section in this book.

4. **Sponsors.** Many marketers realize that the power of 'celebrity status' in an industry sense (not Hollywood) can not only elevate those around the celebrity, but acquire sponsor dollars, too. When you start off, nobody knows who you are. You can use the ABC, CBS or CNN logo on your web site and marketing materials as you book interviews on these shows, write articles or contribute to major publications. Riding on the coat tails of these brands is a great way to establish your credibility. Along this journey, realize that many of these big name brands sponsor smaller venues and databases in order to not only capture new business, but to solidify their image. This works at any level.

As you build a following through your blog and your book, you can begin to approach local, regional and even national companies to sponsor you. My son is passionate about long boarding (longer version of a skateboard). When one of his videos caught the attention of a manufacturer, the manufacturer contacted him about sponsoring his long board team. If a 15-year old can get multi-million dollar corporations to sponsor him, you as a professional businessperson have no excuse.

5. **Trade.** Money certainly talks, but the cash-strapped entrepreneur should always consider barter or trade as a leveraged form of currency. Your cost of goods and services that you provide is always lower than what you charge (you are profitable-aren't you?). Consider trading services with other professionals in lieu of cash. The differential in margin works both ways and makes both parties glad to engage.

Time Saving Tips

Ask any professional or business owner who has been around for any length of time and they should confess that they value their time equal to or more than money. Sure, if you are in start up mode, you have very little of both, but as you grow, you learn that you can always earn more money. Time, however, is a commodity that can never truly be stored, saved or expanded. Personal time is the only finite resource in the world.

Here are a few ideas to maximize your time when you create and market your book.

1. **Dictate.** Many people who embark upon writing a book never finish because it simply takes a Herculean effort to sit down, have no distractions, and craft a high-quality book about themselves and their company. It takes a ton of

time. You should, however, be passionate about your company and mission. You probably light up and are more energetic when you talk about your favorite topic…you! By dictating your thoughts, chapters and ideas into a digital recorder, you can quickly get your thoughts out and even organized by chapter. Send the audio files to a dictation company (see resources) and you should have an editable transcript in a day or two. Compile the files yourself or hire an editor to organize your thoughts for you. A better system, one that pulls relevant, conversational-based content is to be interviewed by a journalist. Their questions and skills at interviewing will create a far superior transcript to work from.

2. **Turn Your Phone Off.** With all respect to Alexander Bell, the phone, text and email interruptions we receive on a daily and hourly basis create such a massive loss of productivity it staggers the mind. Studies have shown that it takes 5-10 times as long to recover from a distraction than the length of the distraction itself. That means, if you are in the "flow" and writing your book, a one-minute phone interruption actually costs you 6 to 11 minutes of lost time. Multiply that by the number of interruptions you receive on a daily basis and do the math. It is far better to have pre-arranged times to receive and place calls. Never keep your email, Facebook, Skype or other communication devices open for people to interrupt you. YOU do the interrupting on your schedule. The average person who lives by these rules effectively picks up 2-3 additional hours of productivity every day!

3. **Touch it once.** You've probably heard this before, but almost no one implements it consistently. When paper, email or a "to do" comes across your desk, vow to only touch it one time. Paper is still a culprit in this digital society. Paper, articles, documents, agreements and other items need not be shuffled about aimlessly. All articles and documents have one of 3 places to go. There are three, not four. Decide to touch the next piece of mail, article or document only ONE time and decide quickly which pile it belongs.

   a. **Trash.** If you don't need it now or in the next few days, recycle it immediately. You don't need a new garbage disposal or new lawn care. If the copy or design doesn't interest you from a marketing perspective, immediately discard it. When you need the deal of a century on a new whiz-bang gizmo, you'll find a deal on your terms and on your time.

   b. **File for later.** This only applies to legal agreements, contracts or articles. When you go through a magazine, don't keep the entire magazine. Rip out the articles that interest you and discard the rest (80-90% ads). Put them in a file marked "Future reading" and read them within 30 days. After 30 days, recycle the entire folder regardless if you have read them or not. If you haven't read it in the past 30 days, its unlikely you will in the next 30.

   c. **Act on it.** Some documents can be acted upon instantly. If there is a report, writing assignment, review or article that needs your attention, DON'T file it for later that day. Read it, act upon it and if appropriate, file it in the circular file when you are done. By putting all of your attention to speed of moving through your paper, you will save a good hour or two per day of moving garbage around or searching for that document you swear you had just last Thursday.

Time is your most valuable resource. Treat it with reverence and respect and you can be 100% more productive. Squander it and you'll continue an existence of frustration and want. As a business owner, you've probably made money and lost money. There aren't many professionals or business owners who haven't earned the badge of honor of a banner year and a drought of cash.

It doesn't matter.

Money can always be earned. Money is the measurement of your business. Time, on the other hand is a resource that is finite. We only can a certain amount and that's it. It can't be borrowed or saved. It is our most precious resource.

List 3 ways you have wasted money in the past

1. _____

2. _____

3. _____

List 3 NEW time management tactics you will use

1. _____

2. _____

3. _____

List 3 ways you will re-invest the time you will save

1. _____

2. _____

3. _____

Chapter 4

Marketing Before You Write

The good news is you can create a book within 90 days if you allocate enough time. The great news is if you DON'T have the time to write, dictate or otherwise go through the learning curve of writing, editing, layout, publishing, marketing and promoting your book, apply for our outcome-based school where your weekly homework becomes your book or give us a call to see if you qualify for our "Do It All For You" service. (See chapter 11).

The bad news is, the success of your book is solely dependent upon the following items. If you are an established business with a phenomenal database, publishers and your accountant are going to love your new strategy for the monetization of your book. Even if you invested $20,000 or more in the development of your book, your credibility, cache and exposure you will garner over the next few years, will easily be worth over $1 million dollars in traditional marketing value. Consider the difference between a $10,000 ½ page ad in a national magazine vs. an article of a page or two. The difference in value is astronomical. The difference is cost is infinity. As an author of your own book, you'll be positioned as an expert instead of a marketer. Being an author also opens you up to contribute to articles in other publications.

"Who has time to write articles for magazines?" I hear you say. Well, there are two sides to that coin. On one hand, consider the alternative $10,000 ad that 90% of the readers gloss over. What did it take you to earn that $10,000 that only a handful of people bother to read? An ad may be pretty, but a high-value article may be read, digested and even passed on to other people, blogs, publications and media channels.

Information or entertainment is what we seek. The ads are there to interrupt our thought process.

Even being quoted in an article is going to give you a better return than a stand-alone advertisement. A few years ago, I contributed to an article in the Seattle times that was picked up by MSN money and Yahoo finance. We received 6 calls directly from those articles. We earned 2 clients worth over $12,000 in business and numerous speaking gigs and hundreds more acknowledgments from prospects, clients and associates. A five minute interview garnered over $12,000 in revenue.

Being part of the media gives you clout.

Many authors erroneously assume that their book has to be completed before they can blog, write or contribute to articles.

The exact opposite is true.

It is far better to begin your journey for recognition today than tomorrow. (Actually yesterday is a better day to start!) If you have a decent database of followers from your office, Facebook, or other channels; good. Keep adding to it.

If you do not have 5,000, 25,000 or more people in your database or contact list, you will need to create one, borrow some and build a following. It is through this list that you will create the connection, trust and revenue for your book and any other products and services you will offer in the future.

It sounds odd to say you need to build a list before you have your book-doesn't it? Why should someone follow you on a consistent basis? What value have you been delivering to them over the previous months or years? If you have not started a blog, it is imperative that you begin immediately.

You needn't be intimidated by Wordpress, programming or the concept of video logs (vlogs) anymore. Creating a high-quality site has never been easier or less expensive. If you don't have the patience or belief that you can, outsource it. But don't get caught in the idea that it requires thousands of dollars to create a decent looking and functional site. There are dozens of choices on each of these categories. If you are lazy or don't want to shop around, I've listed a few popular links. Here is a typical breakdown (average) of the costs:

Reserve web domain: www.godaddy.com	$12
Host domain: www.hostgator.com	$15/mo
Install WordPress: www.fiverr.com	$5
Wordpress templates: www.google.com	Free
Design, adapt the template: www.odesk.com	$50

As you can see, it doesn't take thousands of dollars to create a website anymore. With a few strokes on the keyboard and pocket change, you can have a blog and website up and running in a few hours.

The CRITICAL element of the process isn't the technical side; it is the content. Your content presented on a consistent basis is the key to building a following and creating that loyal tribe of fans that are eager to learn about your story, your message and your company so long as you treat them with respect and be an honorable servant.

What does that mean?

It means that you do NOT laden your content with an overabundance of marketing messages. It is fine to share a few links and to give your contact information. Use this book as an example. My contact information is located on the back cover, in the last chapter and embedded in the other chapters only as it relates to the content. There is an obvious reference as to the service we can provide because for every 100 people who are reading these words, 82 of them WANT to write a book and fewer than 5% of them every will. These are the facts. I am here to serve whom-ever wants help. From our free, no-obligation strategy consultation to a full blown authorship and marketing campaign, we are uniquely qualified to help in any manner.

NOTE: 99% of the people will not take the time to create and publish their book.
Go DIRECTLY to the last chapter and join the 1%
www.authoryourbrand.com

Unfortunately, of those that think they can pull it off on their own, fewer than 5% will finish…ever.

Why?

Because writing, designing, laying out, proofing, publishing and marketing a book is a massive and complex undertaking.

Part of our marketing is THIS book. Your marketing will be YOUR book. There is no such thing as an 'overnight' success. In order to build your reputation as an authority, you'll need to be an expert. Your book will solidify that image, but your ongoing service of good content via your blog, videos, articles and speeches will build your fan base. The sooner you build that base, the more books you will sell when the launch day arrives.

If you don't have a large fan base, don't wait to build it AFTER you write you book, of course. You should be building that base alongside the creation of your book.

You need a blog…right away.

Blog is short for web log and this medium has taken off like a nuclear explosion. Because of the ease and proliferation of blogs, they have become as common as grains of sand on a beach…millions of them look the same and millions more are nothing more than cheap advertising gimmicks.

Blogs that draw and KEEP good quality visitors (called "traffic" in internet-speak) deliver quality content on a consistent basis. The more relevant, interesting and consistent the blog posts are, the higher the blog ranks in the search engines. With millions of blogs and hundreds of thousands of pages on any particular subject, getting your blog post to rank on the first page of Google or Bing is coveted and requires something most people aren't willing to do. Fortunately, our marketing team keeps up with current trends, algorithms and the back door world of technology and search engine optimization. Our clients always rank high for the terms they need. It doesn't happen overnight and it isn't some super-secret method. It takes good old fashioned work, a solid understanding of the process and a commitment to consistency.

There are dozens and dozens of basic principles that pull the blog post to the top of the search engines. Much of the algorithm used is proprietary.

TIP: Give good, fresh, relevant content away consistently for FREE.

However, there are a few basics that can work for you.

1. Consistently blog.

2. Write brief, relevant, and interesting content.

3. Insert strategic keywords in the content and tags.

4. Add pictures, audio and video (called vlogs) to your site.

5. Keep the content fresh and newsworthy.

6. Encourage comments from others.

The more someone quotes YOUR blog and offers to re-blog your post or create a link to your page, the higher your post will rank. People are lazy and tend to search and click on the top results. The next time you search for anything, take a look at the top of the search page. You may see 2,456,439 results for a specific term and almost nobody searches beyond the first 10 entries. We have over a dozen ebooks and courses available on our resource page for members and non-members alike. To preview the downloads, visit www.AuthorYourBrand.com.

OPB

Other people's blogs are another way to gain publicity for yourself. Many blogs allow you to put your "signature" in your comment. This allows the reader of your comment to click on your signature and that link goes directly to your blog. This works ONLY if your comment is relevant, interesting and NOT AN ADVERTISEMENT!

People are marketed to death nowadays so the farther you can remove yourself from self-serving copy the better.

Additionally, choose blogs and stories to comment on that not only ALLOW your signature (many do not) but are highly ranked blogs or websites. Posting a comment on a high-traffic site like Yahoo news will get more views than Bob's chicken farm blog from Pocatello, ID.

In addition to blogging about the message in your book, it is acceptable to add VALUE to other people's websites and blogs. By adding comments with your digital signature you build what are called "backlinks" to your website. Google and other search engines rank sites by the amount of other sites that link to yours. The more people who link to your site, the higher your site appears in the search engine rankings. There are dozens and dozens of other SEO (search engine optimization) tricks and companies who charge thousands for this service.

The more you learn about this, the more confusing it can become. In order to keep it clean and simple, always write what you would want to read. Learn about SEO, but don't become so engrossed in it that you lose sight of the purpose.

The purpose of using the media (digital, print and broadcast) is to elevate your image and brand. See the resource section for more SEO ideas.

List 3 ways you to market yourself and your message prior to publishing your book.

1. _____

2. _____

3. _____

List the numbers of people in your database now

_____

List the number of people you will have in your database a year from now

_____

Chapter 5

Destroying Writer's Block & Other Myths

Choosing to write your book comes in a few flavors. Regardless of the path you choose, you will enlist other professionals to assist you in one way or another. The amount of team members you gather will determine the investment and time necessary to complete your project. In other words, the more professionals you enlist, the less time you will invest to get the project completed.

This does NOT translate to completing the project faster, however. Overseeing the various editors, copywriters, proofreaders, design and graphics professionals can be like herding cats. Rarely does a single person possess all of the necessary skills to create, write, edit, layout, design, proof and publish a high-quality book.

This blueprint will give you several paths to creating your book. No single path is right for everyone and each path may have variations based on your resources and management skills.

Many authors enjoy reading, but when it comes to writing, the task can be overwhelming. Your thoughts generally fly through your head much faster than your fingers can type. Once your thoughts are translated to paper, many authors are their own worst critic and tend to type, retype and edit as they go. This slows the process down even further and many authors have completed a chapter or two, only to scrap the entire concept before they are done. Oftentimes, as you write, your concepts are flushed out; change and either improve or decay.

People suffer from…

- Poor **positioning** (Not positioning the book intelligently)

- Writer's **block** (Inability to write concepts or content)

- Writer's **critic** (Self criticism that stunts creation)

- Writers **time crunch** (Too busy with business to write)

- Writer's **budget** (Not enough capital to hire team members)

- Writer's **skill** (False idea that your words aren't good enough)

Nearly all authors (and some VERY famous best-selling ones) suffer from some or all of these stifling assumptions. The only advice that makes any sense is to recognize these stumbling blocks on your journey and do whatever it takes to reduce or eliminate them.

Your Personal Vision for Your Book

When it comes to book marketing success, the first step is to define your goals for your book. Until you define what publishing success means to you, you can't possibly figure out how to achieve it—or gauge how close you are to achieving it.

Every author has a personal vision of what constitutes publishing success. For one author, publishing success might be signaled by receiving a review in their college alumni newsletter. For another author, publishing success will never be achieved until they have made the New York Times bestseller list.

You will want to ask yourself by what benchmarks you will gauge your book's success—or, conversely, its failure. Now is the time to be very honest and very detailed about just what you hope to achieve through the publication of your book. By doing so you can best determine what publicity, marketing, and sales efforts it will take to achieve your vision.

As you consider your personal vision of publishing success, many factors may come into play—ego, reputation, finances, professional standing, altruism, personal legacy, etc. You might want to consider your goals as falling into one of three categories: personal, financial, or professional.

Benchmarks are your way of gauging if you have achieved your goals. In other words, what does achieving your goals actually look like?

Possible Benchmarks

- Receive a specific number of reviews on Amazon.com.

- Reach a certain number of copies sold.

- Appear on a specific television program.

- Book speaking engagements related to your book's topic.

Consider what your goals for your book are. Then, list them along with the specific benchmarks you will use to gauge whether or not you have achieved your goals.

Identifying Your Book's Key Marketing Message

When someone asks you what your book is about, what they really want to know is, "Why should I read your book?" In other words, they want to hear a compelling argument. They want to know what your book's key marketing message is.

What goes into a key marketing message?

A number of qualities factor into a book's key marketing message, including:

- Subject matter

- Value and benefit to the reader

- The author's qualifications

- Superiority or uniqueness compared to other titles

To identify your book's key marketing message, begin by completing the following exercises:

1. Category

In what section or sections would you expect to find your book in a bookstore or library? In other words, what category or categories does your book fall into? As you consider this question, you might wish to refer to the categories used by Amazon.com or the BISAC subject headings sheet in the Resources section at the end of this workbook. Include all of the subject headings or categories that seem relevant to your book.

2. Ranking Categories by Relevance

Most books fall into more than one category. For example, a book written about successful female entrepreneurs could be found under subject categories such as "business," "entrepreneurship," "careers," "women's studies," or even "self-help." A factual account chronicling the murder of an important historical figure could be categorized as "true crime," "history," or "biography."

If your book fits into more than one category, determine which category you feel is the most relevant to your book, then list the rest of the categories in descending order of importance:

1.

2.

3.

Features/Benefits

Your book serves a purpose—it offers some sort of benefit to the potential reader. Perhaps it solves a problem, meets a desire, informs or entertains—but there was a purpose behind your decision to write and publish your book.

In order to effectively market your book to your intended audience, you will have to identify and articulate to potential readers what benefits they will be able to gain by buying and reading your book.

Begin by imagining the potential reader of your book and why they might seek out your book in the first place. For example:

The potential reader of my book is desperate to lose weight, but is frustrated by complicated diet plans that take forever to show results.

Next, isolate the features in your book that will help the reader. For example:

My book provides easy-to-follow, step-by-step instructions guaranteed to help the reader lose 30 pounds in three weeks.

Finally, describe the benefit that your reader will likely experience as a result of reading your book. For example:

Reader will lose weight in an easy and efficient manner.

State the problems, issues and/or desires that your book was created to help readers with, along with the features in your book that meet or resolve these problems, issues and/or desires. Then provide the benefits that readers of your book will likely experience. Be specific.

Reader's Problem/Issue/Desire

Book's Feature   Benefit to Reader

1.

2.

3.

4.

5.

6.

7.

8.

9.

10.

The bottom line is your MUST clearly answer these two questions:

1. Why does someone want to read my book?

2. Who are they? (age, situation, lifestyle, problem, issue, etc.)

The more detailed you can be with these two questions, the more successful your book and subsequent product and service offerings will be. With proper positioning, even a mediocre book can do well from a marketing perspective. Creating a mediocre book isn't a goal, mind you, but tends to trump content in many cases.

With great positioning AND a high-quality book, you can make a difference.

But what about writer's block, editing as you write, time and all the other stumbling blocks along the way?

Here are a few ideas to help:

Writers block

When you are faced with a blank slate, take advantage of it. Don't over think your ideas, concepts, history or values. Just start jotting down notes. Leonardo DaVinci's greatest creations were not exclusive to the Sistine Chapel…some of his most innovative ideas were concepts and simple notes in his journal.

Here is the perfect cure for writer's block. Most creative people have MORE than one book inside of them. Go ahead and write down 5,10 or even 20 or more titles, ideas and concepts that you have. When you compile notes, write or dictate, you may jump from idea to idea. That is not schizophrenic, that is CREATIVE! Simply label each note, dictation or idea by color or concept. Set up file folders (real or digital) for each topic, story or concept separately.

When you are "blocked" or stuck on one book, immediately pick up your notes or files from one of your other topics and let you mind wander, create or even destroy! The more you let your thoughts free, the more they will come to you faster than you can write!

Writer's critic

Rarely does a creative work have only a single draft. Your manuscript WILL be edited. How much editing has absolutely no reflection on the end result or impact you will have on your audience. There are books that have been edited for weeks and those that have been "in process" for years. Even best selling "how to" books have updated editions and improvements as the author adds to his work and as the environment evolves. Notably, Robert Allen's' best selling book, "Nothing Down" had several editions including "Nothing Down for the 90's" and "Nothing Down for the 2000's".

Writers time crunch

How do you eat an elephant? "One bite at a time" goes the famous quote. Writing can be tedious and extremely time consuming. Even a simple, short book cannot be created in a day. If you choose to create something special, give it the time it is due. Don't fixate on the monumental task of creating 130, 150 or 200 pages. So many writers become frustrated with the huge task of completing they never even start. Don't fall into that trap. By simply writing a single page or two a day, your book can be crafted in just a few months. Begin.

Writers budget

With the proliferation of freelancers across the globe and the dozens of self-publishing companies available, it is no wonder that MORE books are being created every year. Less than 10 years ago, hiring an editor, copywriter, graphic artist, and all the other people necessary would easily be a 5 or 6 figure enterprise. Simply hiring a decent ghostwriter could run you over $100,000! There are plenty of freelancer websites where you can hire and assemble all the people necessary from across the globe to pull your work together on nearly any budget. (See resources) Perhaps the most encouraging development is the world of self-publishing and on-demand publishing. With the click of a mouse, nearly anyone can have a soft cover or hardbound book printed and shipped anywhere in the world!

Writer's skill

See above! If you are awake and can talk, you can create a book. You don't even have to have a great command of language! One of my friends, Ron Shimony, is an Israeli immigrant and his book, "Ron for Your Life" is an excellent example of how a person with broken English and a terrific editor, proof reader and copy editor can work together to create a great book. Don't EVER concern yourself with your skill as a writer. The only requirement to be an author is the desire to publish a book-period. Using any of the 3 methods outlined in this blueprint will give you a book that you can be proud of and can elevate your status in any profession.

There are three distinct methods to creating your book. With a good amount of time, money and massaging, each of these methods probably has infinite variables. It doesn't matter which method you choose to get started. The most IMPORTANT thing to do is to simply start. You may start on one path and switch to another. There is no crime in starting to write you book out…becoming frustrated and hiring someone to finish it for you. Likewise, if you start banging that keypad every day for a week…develop writers block or become time strapped and choose to record a bunch of chapters that is also acceptable. There are no rules to this game except that your creation will never occur without your leadership.

You must start and finish the project.

Lets breakdown each method into easy and manageable steps. Before you begin, there is one foundational concept that will save you time…a ton of time.

Many authors tend to be a bit picky about their works. Of course they have pride and don't want to produce any subpar works. However, no matter what you create, it will ALWAYS be a process. Your words rarely come out the first time, go to print and are read. Revisions, editing and proofing are all necessary steps that must occur. The BIG mistake many people make, however, is that they edit while they are writing. Correcting spelling, phrases or layouts as you write slows your process down and worse, it dilutes your creativity. The lesson is difficult to accomplish. As we write, we are reading what we wrote and if it looks funky, we want to fix it. Don't fall into this trap. Write or speak fast and furious. It will actually save you a huge amount of time.

Version 1: Write it one page at a time

As the example above explains, sitting down and writing a book can be perceived as a daunting task. Don't succumb to the temptation to edit as you go. You will definitely stunt your creativity and slow the process.

Writing can be tedious because your brain thinks faster than it can type. Don't slow your thinking down! Speed of thought can be a wonderful thing…as you trust your intuition, it becomes sharper and your ideas will actually come out clearer if you let the mistakes happen and ignore the context of your thoughts.

Of course, no book of any substance or quality can be written in a day, so don't worry about the speed with which you write or the amount of pages you are creating.

When you consider great business book like Stephen Covey's *7 Habits for Highly Effective People* or Michael Gerber's *The Tipping Point* keep in mind that these books contained exhaustive research, thought and conceptualization. Many years were invested to provide you the distilled knowledge in a 200-page book.

By the same token, consider the essence of *The Tipping Point*. The book is about a single concept! In fact, you could simply explain the concept on a single flash card! The problem is, nobody would pay $20 for a flash card or even 7 of them!

Books are highly valued BECAUSE of the thought you put behind it. You do not need 10 years of research and a Ph.D. to create your masterpiece, but don't ignore the fact that 200, 150 or even a 90-page book will have significant content in those pages and your thoughts, ideas and perspective will be important to showcase.

Taking your time is an asset, not a liability.

How do you eat an elephant?

One bite at a time.

It doesn't matter if you are business owner, professional or stay at home mom. YOU have only 24 hours in a day and probably don't have "spare" time to put into a book.

Being patient with yourself not only eases any potential frustration with the time it requires, but also gives your creation a better chance of being of good quality. Rushed projects rarely compare to ones that have been thoroughly researched, proofed and crafted.

CREATION TIP: If you can bang out a page in 10, 15 or even 30 minutes, budget ONE block of time each day to create and dump your content onto a disk. Eating your elephant "one bite at a time" by creating only 1 or 2 pages per day can give you enough content to become a real book in just a few months. Patience always wins.

Version 2: Get someone to write it for you

Ghostwriters are like wines, some are inexpensive and others are prohibitive. I have seen quotes for as little as $1500 to as high as $300,000 to create a book. The quality between these two is as large as the price.

Regardless of the budget you have to hire a ghostwriter,

keep in mind you will need a slew of other professionals to create your book. Notably, you will need:

1. Concept editor. This person can review your content, organize it in a cohesive manner and has experience with published books. They may or may not have proof reading as an additional skill set.

2. Proof reader. This type of editor corrects for grammar, spelling and punctuation. Microsoft word can never be trusted for this function. You need a set of human eyes to verify you don't sound ignorant.

3. Layout artist. Many people judge a book by its cover. Once they open it up, people scan headlines, bullet points and paragraphs. The clearer your book is organized, the more people will engage and the more copies you will sell.

4. Graphic artist. People DO judge a book by its cover. Even interior pictures, graphs and website will need a person who understands and is proficient with design, art and composition.

5. Publisher. Traditional publishing is a completely separate topic and in the glossary, you will find some excellent sources for getting an agent, publisher and the marketing machine you will need to create a platform for your book and make the publisher a ton of money (That is what they are banking on…not your genius book, I'm afraid). You may start out with self-publishing your book and there are different levels of involvement available to you from simply printing all the way up to five and six

figure marketing fees to firms that will take your book to the masses.

Your first hire will be a ghostwriter. The other people you put on your team may come from referrals or other sources available to you. Let's start with where and how you hire someone to tell your story. Here are your steps:

1. Do your research on WHY someone would want to read your book.

2. Have a clear idea (examples are helpful) of what your book is about.

3. Give YOUR differentiating angle (there isn't a topic that hasn't been covered).

4. Post a project "Ghostwriter needed" on several places and ask for samples.

5. Interview your prospective writer based on:

   a. Their experience

   b. Their examples

   c. Their ability to capture your spirit, voice and message

6. It is customary to give them a non-refundable deposit to start work.

7. It is also acceptable to have a revision or two after the first draft.

8. Ghostwriters traditionally do NOT do design, layout or editing.

   (See appendix for resources)

Version 3: Talk your book

Of all the methods to create a book, this one may be the easiest to pull off. Unlike a strict ghostwriting assignment where the ghostwriter must collect a myriad of notes, files and interviews from you, the "talk your book" concept will be fast, clear and a bit more economical if you follow the examples below.

The Concept

Before you can digitally record your book, you still need to be a bit organized. Many professionals have a vague idea of what their book is about, but do not have the structure in place to pull it together. Create a basic concept on what you'd like to communicate. Here are a few ideas:

- **Story.** Make your book a linear progression of your life's journey. Having someone interview you and asking you the RIGHT questions is critical. Simply recalling your past from memory, you will leave out juicy details and may not have a theme that someone can learn from. "Tuesdays with Maury" is a best seller that followed a simple interview format on a man's life and his perspective on dying.

- **Passion.** You may be passionate about your hobby, business or a value. Talking about that passion will be easier to some than others. Most passionate people won't be at a loss for words when discussing their favorite subject. The outline or framework you choose to discuss in your passion can take any shape you desire. It can be full of photographs, lessons, or "how to."

- **Life Lessons.** If you have life experience (hint: we all do) that has shaped your situation, someone else can probably learn from it. Your past challenges and how you overcame death, divorce, cancer or other perceived tragedy could inspire others. Or perhaps you have had a series of unfortunate events that can be retold in a humorous manner. In either case, the lessons you learned from your experiences in life can be a great framework for a book.

- **Business.** You are unique. Even if you own a franchise that 1,000 other business people own, your path to success is YOUR story. Do you have 7 principles that have guided you? Is there a core value that you apply to your professional, personal and spiritual life? Many books are really about a single concept and that concept is simply peeled apart like an onion for the reader to digest, reflect and learn from.

Here is a simple and highly effective method to start (and finish) your book in record time. Credit for this method is given to my friend, Craig Duswalt.

1. Tape 10 single pieces of paper to your wall.

2. Write a single word, sentence or concept on each piece of paper.

3. Get a digital recorder and talk about each concept as thoroughly as possible.

4. Send the recordings to a transcription service.

5. Organize, cut, paste or edit the transcription or hire someone else to do it.

6. Voila! Your book is ready for layout, design and proofing!

NOTE: This is a great system to start with. Over the years of working with hundreds of best selling authors, journalists and content marketers, if you can afford it, hire a professional interviewer to go through your outline and interview you. The perspective they bring and the skills at getting to the core intent of your notes will be night and day to you simply giving your monologue.

Writing your book is just the beginning. In order to leverage your message, creating a platform, website and enlisting joint venture partners can catapult your career, brand and image. Be sure to keep up your momentum.

Writing your book can be one of the most gratifying experiences of your life.

The moment your book is completed and those first copies show up at your door will be a moment you will never forget.

The first positive review you receive from someone other than your mom will do more to your self-confidence than finishing a marathon or winning an award at work. Publishing your book will put you in the top 1% of the respected professionals in the world.

You are an author.

List 10 ideas you have for a book or series

1. _____

2. _____

3. _____

4. _____

5. _____

6. _____

7. _____

8. _____

9. _____

10. _____

Chapter 6

"Detail-itis" & Other Diseases

DO NOT EDIT AS YOU WRITE!

*T*his bears repeating! If you fall into the trap of editing as you create, you are engaging both the left and right sides of your brain. The creative side starts, and then stops as the other side corrects the spelling, grammar or layout. Resist the urge to correct anything during the creative process. The amount of time you save can be 100, 200 even 500% what most people spend as they type-correct-type-proof-etc.

Resist that urge and your creativity will flow faster and with less effort. You will have plenty of opportunity and resources to edit and proof after you "data dump" all of your thoughts, ideas and content onto the page or recorder. If you find yourself correcting yourself and can't stop, go ahead and employ method 3 to finish your book. Correcting what you say takes less time than what you type.

DON'T DO THIS   DO THIS INSTEAD

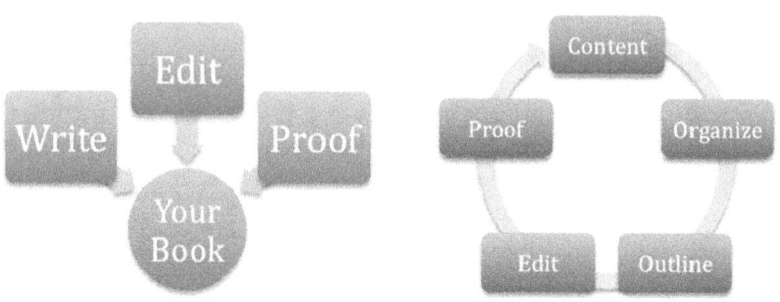

Finding an editor is as simple as going to YOUR favorite books and looking up the acknowledgements from the author. He/she should give credit to his editor. Next, Google their name along with the book title and you should be able to find them.

Don't be shy about going for a high profile editor. They are worth their weight in gold. If you can't afford them now, use the freelance links in the resource section instead and stay in touch with them. After your sales climb, you can revisit hiring a "celebrity" editor to make the 2nd edition of your book a best seller!

When it comes to the process flow of editing, there are several areas. Do these out of order and you can add weeks or years to your undertaking. Do them in order may seem a bit odd, but the end result will be a flow that will allow you to crank out content and copy like a professional.

1. **Content Research.** The more research you do before you write the better. Don't concern yourself too much with the title or abstract at this point. Take your basic premise and

search similar topics, stories and examples of who else is talking about it. Compile a folder of notes and focus on the content.

2. **Market Research.** As you uncover content that relates to your topic, you will come across good copy, bad books and interesting methods that other people are using to market and promote their message. Keep these ideas and strategies in a separate folder when able. You can probably ignore any marketing strategy that was "new" in the 80's or 90's. Keep current. Look for cutting edge content. The bottom line for any marketing will be how well you connect with your clients.

3. **Data Dump.** Write, dictate and jot down your notes, thoughts and concepts that will comprise your intellectual property. If you are a linear thinker, go ahead and write out the chapter titles and bullet points to support each. DO NOT worry if some of your thoughts overlap or repeat. Repetition is necessary for learning and when you repeat a concept in a different manner, you drill into the head of your reader the importance of your thoughts.

4. **Organization.** Now the editing starts. Don't worry about formatting, spacing or the number of pages. As you organize your thoughts, your focus should be on the pace, cadence and rhythm of our words. Cut, paste, delete, add and organize your headings, examples and words so that they make sense. You will end up reading and re-reading your manuscript many times over. DO NOT correct grammar or spelling if you can help it.

5. **Grammar and spelling.** Use spell check and turn on the grammar checker, too. Some people are comfortable using slang in their books (me) and others are not. It is your choice and is dependent upon your target audience. After you spell check your book, go through and re-read the sentences, points and flow. This will be the last time you read it word for word before you attack the layout. Be sure the paragraphs are crisp and brief. Some people skim as they read and paragraphs with too many sentences are harder to read for many people.

6. **Layout & graphics.** If you are adding any photos, images, drawings or graphics, add these last. When you do, it will affect the formatting of your book. Adjust them as necessary so that the pages flow evenly. Re-size photos to fit within the margins of your book.

7. **Page numbers.** After you layout is complete, you can go through the book and do a page count, noting how many pages are in each chapter. Go back to the table of contents and insert the appropriate amount of pages per chapter. This is important for marketing as well as flow. Readers often want to revisit a certain section and your roadmap (table of contents) allows them a quick way to reference any part of your book.

8. **Cover.** Yup, we all judge a book by its cover. Sadly, this along with the title can make or break a book. Unless you are a graphic artist, hire this function out. You'll save endless hours of frustration and many designers charge a few hundred to as little as $50 to design a cover for you. Do

yourself a favor and DON'T skimp on this part. The packaging of your book (cover) is vital. When it comes to titles, people love a play on words, controversy or engaging titles. Visit bookstores online and offline and see what catches your eye. Ask yourself why it catches your attention and make note of the feeling you had when you read a captivating title.

9. **Proof.** After you are all done with your content, design, layout, cover and title, you have to have your book proofed. Send it to an English teacher, a proofreader or your mom, but get it read by someone who is extremely picky. Fred Gleek purposely does NOT use proofreaders and simply sends out a few hundred copies of the first run of his books. Suffice to say, there are always a few dozen people who find his mistakes, call his attention to it and correct it for him. I sort of like this from a marketing and budget standpoint. Anytime you can engage your clients, you are building a relationship; even if they are criticizing you!

10. **ISBN.** Each book has to have an ISBN or catalog number with the library of congress. With over 1.5 million new books being published annually, there will be more that 2 that share a similar title. Visit www.isbn.org and order a number for your book (or 10 for your book series!) You should also get a bar code to place on the back cover. That will make it easy for your distributors to sell, track and ship your books. These are also available at www.isbn.org. If you are going to use Amazon for distribution, they can provide your ISBN and barcode at no charge.

Do these steps in a linear fashion and resist the temptation to edit as you write. You will definitely save your most valuable asset…time.

Don't forget to hire professionals to assist you with any or all of these steps. Treat your book as the large enterprise it can be. Doing it all yourself is a crazy as building your current business all by yourself. Quite frankly, it's impossible. Even solo entrepreneurs have vendors that handle printing, bookkeeping, and sourcing of products. Doctors don't make their own medicine and truckers don't build their own vehicles.

As a soon-to-be successful author, you will create and rely upon a team to move your brand to the spotlight. Don't wait until you are frustrated and confused…get busy and contact all the freelancers you need to pull off this project. If you prefer a "one-stop" approach to this entire concept, drop us a line at doug@dougcrowe.com and we'll explore working together. You can start off by registering for our free newsletter at www. authoryourbrand.com.

 Socializing Social Media

*T*here is a significant difference between information, knowledge and wisdom. All three are necessary, but how you invest your time in acquiring and filtering knowledge is critical.

You'd have to be stranded on a deserted island if you don't know the absolute exponential opportunity with what has been called Web 2.0. The proliferation of Facebook, YouTube, Google+ and Twitter along with hundreds of other social networking sites has revolutionized the manner in which people are connecting, sharing buying. If you don't adapt and grow with this wave, you will surely be lost in the outdated strategies of yesteryear.

These web properties are using a human beings curiosity about others along with the ego of self in order to build online communities like never before. A few years ago, chat rooms and online forums were all the rage. Those faceless, linear portals gave people a chance to share and be heard…one at a time.

In fact, as I write this, Google+ is making headway as a social networking community. New players come into the mix every day.

Facebook and YouTube put a dramatic spin on the concept of community by allowing you to attach a face to a name. It isn't simply placing your profile picture next to a post or a blog entry. The Facebook and YouTube phenomenon allows anyone to not only be a TV star, but to share what you are up to and thinking with the rest of the world.

Like slowing down when passing the scene of an accident, for some reason, humans can't stop watching what is happening to others; good bad or innocuous.

How does all of this social networking relate to you, the new author?

Easy.

You have, for the first time, the ability to connect with your fans, readers, customers and friends worldwide in the blink of an eye. This means that authors cannot only build larger fan bases across borders quickly and inexpensively, but it can be done for next to nothing.

There are dozens of books and sources on using these three giants to place your brand in the public eye and develop the loyal fan base you need as an author. See our resource guide for a list of books and resources that you can use today. LinkedIn is another property that needs to be addressed. Largely business-based, your profile and blog should also be featured on that site along with the big three social ones.

For the distilled, day-by-day outline on how to use these 3 portals, follow the bouncing ball. This information may be obsolete by the time you read this, so check on our website for updates.

1. **Facebook Fan Page.** Start a "fan" page on Facebook. They are now called "Like" pages. I am going to refer to them as your business page. The benefit to these pages is there is no limit to the number of friends you can have on this page. (Facebook currently caps the number of personal friends at 5,000)

2. **Buttons.** Put a "like" button on your website. Be sure that the button allows visitors to post comments on your blog and connect with your fan page on Facebook.

3. **Tweet Daily.** Set up an automated twitter account using any number of service providers that can "pre-load" a months' worth of 'tweets' and broadcast them daily to your friends (www.hootsuite.com). Be sure the service you use posts the tweets to Facebook and a few other networking sites of your choosing. Make the tweets useful for others. Learning that you are doing the dishes might appeal to a few people, but sharing an interesting story or link to an article will be more useful for your business, brand and book.

4. **Video Log.** Start a weekly video blog or "vlog" as they are known. It doesn't matter if you are shy or don't have a fancy camera. People do business with other people. All things being equal, we would rather buy from a person than a cor-

poration, so casual and familiar is more important than slick and professional. Deliver relevant and short content (2-3 minutes is best) of your very best stuff. Encourage people to share the links with their friends.

5. **Squeeze Page.** Set up a separate page that's sole purpose is to give the visitor a MASSIVE value in exchange for their name and email. You've seen these done poorly and some done well. My favorite method is to actually give your very best content away for free without asking for any contact info. Being a "go-giver" as my friend and mentor Bob Burg aptly coined in his book means you give value first, without expecting anything in return. In so doing, when you do ask for contact information, the recipient can expect the same or greater value with your email, video or web content. Give away a 15-20 minute tutorial, white paper or eBook that is content rich and marketing light. The next interaction you have with that person will earn you the right to ask for their contact information.

In all of your social media strategy, it is important to have a focus and a destination. Don't post garbage on Facebook or You-Tube simply to post content. Give away stories, information, education and add personality to what you do. Drive your viewers to your blog, vlog or fan page consistently and keep your marketing and "sales" copy to a minimum. People are extremely savvy nowadays and can smell an embedded pitch. The more you give selflessly, the greater return you will realize on a long-term basis. The more you can start a conversation and encourage responses, feedback and a sharing of ideas, the better.

In order to have your book reach as many people as possible, many authors employ social media managers to create Facebook content, tweet relevant links and interact with your fans. Do this only under your personal supervision and be sure to employ an intern or person who is social media proficient. You don't have time to train someone, especially if you are a newbie yourself. Get help and focus on the tasks only you can do.

Book Launch & Social Media Blueprint

The following book launch system includes strategies and tactics to launch a book and brand. Traditionally, the company's profit comes from speaking, products, joint ventures and the marketing of additional products to the buyers and readers of the book. Net revenue from book sales is a bonus. First and foremost, the mission of the book is to establish the author as an expert.

The overall BRAND is supported by 4 interlocking modalities that all support and bring the reader back to the book. The modalities include:

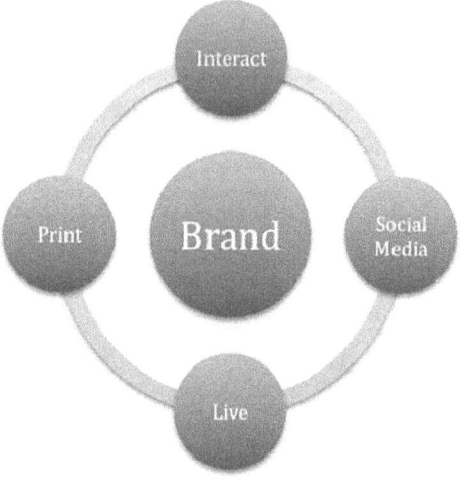

- **Print Media** (press releases, newspaper clippings, flyers, the book, etc.)

- **Online Media** (Social Media, blogs, websites, youtube, forums, etc.)

- **Interaction** (Contests, games, conversations)

- **Live** (Speaking, telephone calls)

The modalities are supported by a combination of:

- **Social Proof** (Give Credibility to the message)

- **Content** (Specific benefits in various forms)

- **Value** (What the partner, affiliate, supporter or customer exchanges)

All messages should include social proof and "service-first" content. With this combination, all touch points stand out from "sales clutter." The brand will become instantly recognized so long as these two aspects are kept in front of the reader (subtly or overtly).

The following campaign includes both pre-launch, launch and campaign tactics that will insure not only a successful book launch, but an evergreen business with a loyal following, provided the marketer provides more value to the reader than is asked for in exchange.

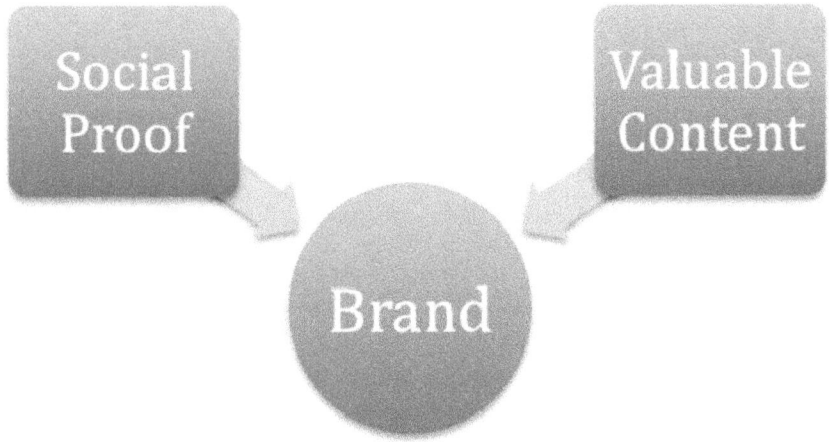

 Auto Responders Stink!

INTERRUPTION MARKETING
(target or broadcast)

*I*n a world of coupons, giveaways and "come-on's" the marketing landscape is cluttered and noisy. Businesses and marketers scramble for new business through "interruption" marketing and reaching out to everyone. By being "in your face" everywhere you go, interruption marketing forces the message upon the consumer.

It doesn't matter if the marketing is broacast to everyone or targeted to a narrow niche. Interrupting someone has always been considered rude, regardless of how clever the message is.

A more sustainable and painless strategy (for both the customer and the purveyor) is **education-based** marekting.

EDUCATION-BASED MARKETING

In the online world, people search for what they want to learn and what they want to buy. Interrupting a person's search to learn about braaces with an offer for teeth whitening confuses their thought process.

With education-based marketing, we deliver EXACTLY what the searcher is looking for. More importantly, the information is delivered at the proper TIME the person is searching for it.

Education-based Marketing	Traditional Marketing
- Informs	- Influences
- Educates	- Manipulates
- Customer asks to buy	- Provider asks to sell

At any particular time, a consumer is in one of three stages of action. By communicating to the consumer "when" they are, not necessarily "who" they are, we engage them more genuinely, with more trust and with equal respect regardless of where they are in the chain of events. The three basic stages are:

1. **Research.** This can include general information, competitive pricing or comparing alternatives.

2. **Decision.** The person has decided to act. They have completed their research and are shopping for the best value.

3. **Buy.** Time to make the purchase. For online and offline purchasing the easier and safer it is to buy, the less friction there is for the sale.

4. **Post Sale.** This is where many marketers blow it. The lifetime value of a customer can be 10 to 100X more than the initial sale.

RESEARCH PHASE

A. Deliver the quality educational content they are looking for, thereby establishing your brand as a trusted and credible source. By focusing on education and NOT selling, your brand rises above the clutter, noise and obvious come on's of traditional interruption marketing.

B. When they are ready to buy, they will naturally come to us because of our credibility and positioning as the expert and trusted resource.

C. We capture contact information and insert the lead into an automated funnel system that continues to EDUCATE & build credibility.

D. Using the book, blog, FB, Google+ and twiter INTERACTION along with a series of FREE video tutorials we position Ageless Human and Gordon as a highly credible source of fitness and health education.

DECISION PHASE

A. Deliver the compelling argument that causes them to select us. This content is specifically pre-set for those who have expressed and interest in taking action.

B. Embedded in this stream of content are offers to take a "test drive" or a high-quality mechanism to start a conversation and build a relationship based on a "no-brainer" transaction. This becomes two-way communication and sale within the 2nd or 3rd contact point.

BUYING PHASE

A. Always make it very easy to do business with. Money back guarantees on all digital products, one-click ordering and a high level of customer care will generate referrals and repeat customers.

B. It is always easier to keep a current customer than to acquire a new one. With a heavy emphasis on a membership and continuity program (Bexsi and infomercial sales) The lifetime value of a customer can exceed thousands of dollars.

POST-BUYING PHASE

A. It can cost 5-10X more money to acqire a new customer as opposed to servicing an existing one. Focusing customer service inside of a membership program can make keeping clients a profit center as opposed to an expense.

B. Most businesses will tell you that the best form of advertising is referrals, but less than 1 in 100 have a clear, measurable and system-based plan for acquiring those referrals.

The more you position yourself as the credible and authoritative voice in a sea of obvious (and sometimes obnoxious) marketers, the more trust, credibility and long-term clients we will have.

To that end, the campaign designed STARTS with education and consumer information. Next steps will capture the leads and place each person onto the education/relationship conveyor belt depending on where they are in the research-decision-buying process.

In order to serve those who are ready to buy now with those who will buy later, a multi-phase lead capture system must be installed in both the online and offline tactics for your brand. By meeting people where they are, the practice can accomplish ALL of its goals with a singular campaign.

Automated drip campaigns work best when you have one clear objective. Campaigns can be sent daily, weekly, or monthly and can be used to keep your brand top of mind when the subscribers are ready to take action. Your practice can set up drip campaigns for specialized holiday campaigns, monthly invoices or annual subscription notices, or anything that keeps their subscribers informed and interested in their organization.

But the real power lies in the ability to create closed loop marketing messages. The concept is simple - communicate a message to a group of subscribers and send your next message based on their reactions and responses.

Subscribers who click on a specific link in the message get one email, the ones who click on a different link get another, and the ones who do nothing get yet another. This takes drip campaigns to the next level as it goes beyond branding and moves into the sales realm. Instead of just pushing content out you design specific paths to lead subscribers through the sales cycle based on their behavior and needs.

All of my clients are encouraged to utilize this "closed loop" messaging system. We've all been insulted by marketers who continue to treat us like prospects after we became customers. I've unsubscribed to countless newsletters because of this cold, informal and faceless automation.

Be different. Be personal and invest some extra time in speaking to each of your prospects and customers "when" they are in addition to "who" they are.

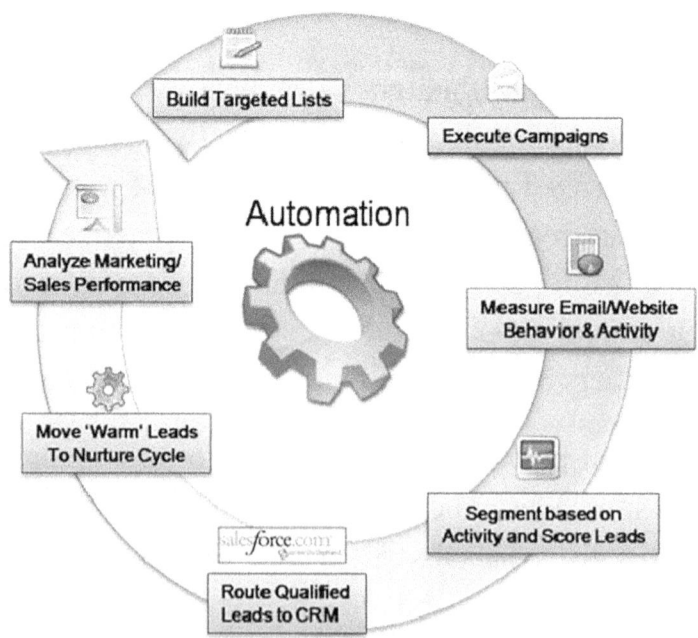

Chapter 9

The Oprah Effect: Get Booked on TV & Radio as the Expert Author

*S*pread your book across the country at the speed of sound! Becoming a popular guest on radio and TV shows worldwide takes consistent effort and a unique message. You may not want to speak publicly about your book, but people want to hear about it! If you are nervous about public speaking, there are "work-arounds" for that. Contact us at www.authoryourbrand. com for a free report on how to be a smooth and engaging guest.

For most business owners and professionals, the idea of talking about their vocation, avocation or passion comes effortlessly. Your book is merely the beginning of a game-changing shift. Getting press will be the start of something new and wonderful for most of you. You may not make it on "The Today Show" right away, but many first time authors have. The good news is, with just a little push on a consistent basis, you can get enough media exposure to accomplish your primary goal of becoming a recognized expert in your field and elevating you and your brand higher than your competition.

Before you map out your campaign strategy, understand that public relations (PR) has changed...dramatically.

They dynamic of PR in just the past few years has not simply changed, but has transformed to such a degree that publicists worldwide who have NOT made the shift are going out of business in record numbers. Historically, there used to be 3 TV stations a dozen radio stations and a single newspaper in town. If you wanted to get publicity, there were gatekeepers and an entire industry of agents, producers, and PR firms whose sole mission was to get THEIR clients their precious 5 minutes of fame. That was the system for decades.

It's all but gone now.

Instead there are 500 different TV channels being delivered via satellite, cable and the web. There are over 1,000 radio stations broadcasting within your 1-mile radius. Many of these are available on satellite radio and many thousands more are available on the Internet. Print media?...forget it. Newspapers and magazines are not dead...yet. With an unlimited supply of blogs and online media sources, there is no limit to the number of outlets for the printed word.

A few years ago there may have been only 20-100 media outlets to focus on. Today the number is actually infinite.

Where do you begin?

Follow the outline and details below on taking your book and media campaign to any level you desire. Your first objective is NOT to sell a ton of books from doing interviews, but to bring credibility to you and your book. It is this credibility that will create a surge of MORE media attention and future sales of your book, seminars, products and services. Your book and its message is the conduit. Making a million from your book may be a long-term goal, but you don't need to sell a million copies to make a million dollars! (NOTE: See our report called "Archimedes Lever" for more information on leveraging your book to making millions with your brand)

Here is an outline that can allow you to get the media exposure you desire, elevate your brand, sell more books, products and seamlessly add exceptional value to your business.

A) Create a book about you, your brand, message or business.

B) Use your book's message as a conduit to leverage the media.

C) Establish yourself as an expert.

D) Leverage national brands to elevate you to celebrity status.

E) Sell more products and services with less marketing and sales costs.

The end result is to make more money and create a better lifestyle for you and your family. Throwing money at marketing, sales campaigns, etc. can be exhausting and risky!

Using the media not only is FREE but the credibility of being a guest on a radio show has 100X the value of being an advertiser on the show. It requires more work, but less money!

The outline for utilizing the media as your marketing partner requires some effort, of course.

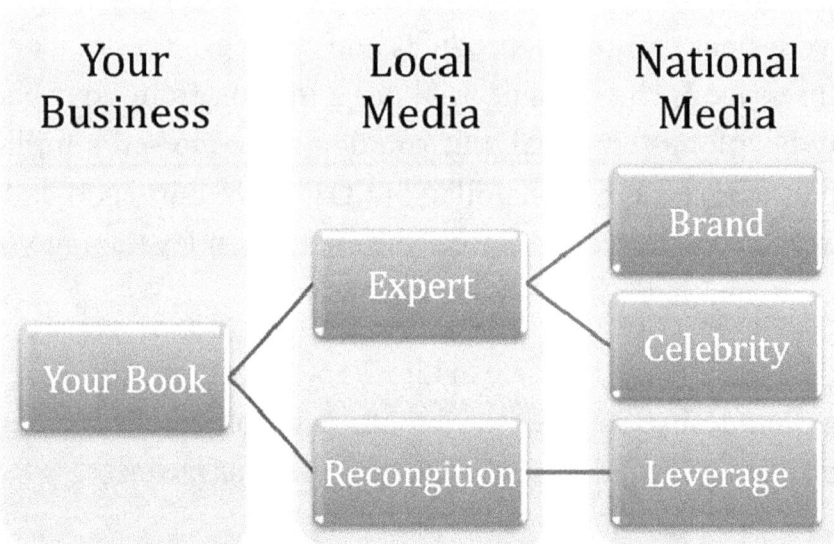

Be a Guest on the Radio

One of the easiest methods to gaining media exposure is to do radio interviews. Getting booked on the radio isn't as difficult as it may appear. Consider the fact that there are thousands of radio stations across the country and nearly all of them are on the air 24 hours a day! That is a ton of content that has to be filled every day and producers are always looking for new and interesting guests to feature.

The producer's job is NOT to make you famous. Their job

is to keep their listeners interested in what you have to say in order for them NOT to tune out during a commercial. That's it!

Therefore, the better you become at doing compelling, interesting and value-added interviews, the more you will be booked on shows. Many authors will do interviews over and over again on the same station IF they know how to make the host of the show look good.

Of course, producers and hosts of these programs realize you are doing the interview for publicity and they almost always give you a chance to plug your book and/or company. If they forget to ask, it is not considered bad form to simply interject your website at the end of the interview.

You will need the following items to start your radio campaign:

1. Bio on you and your experience

2. Compelling headline and story concept

3. Book sample and book overview

Once you have the materials you can contact radio producers or have them search for you (Both is good!) Register for Steve Harrison's Reporter Connection for media who are seeking guests. He also has a trade journal called, RTIR that producers use to seek out guests. (See resource guide) Steve not only puts your ad in front of thousands of radio producers, his staff helps you create your ad copy.

Once you start doing a few interviews, always get audio copies of the interview and the logo from the station. Get permission to put both on your website. See the resource guide for a list of sources of radio producers who want to share your story!

Blog Radio

Broadcast radio still has more prestige than Internet radio, but popular bloggers and some broadcast personalities are making the move to put their shows online. Don't overlook this outlet for getting media exposure.

In fact, many authors have used this venue to start their OWN radio program! While this may seem like starting a whole new business (it can be), you could always have a week-ly radio show where you were the host and interviewed a guest each week on a topic that was important to you, your industry or demographic.

Being a radio host would add to your credibility and by in-terviewing people in your industry, you add to your own brand along the way.

Once you start interviewing others, post those audio files on your website. When your guests do the same, exchange links to increase your SEO. If you want to add further SEO, transcribe the interviews and allow your website visitors to read or download them.

Video and TV

Television has changed forever. This visual medium has gone for a half a dozen channels, to thousands of satellite and cable stations. With the proliferation of YouTube and dozens of other video sites, the actual number of "channels" is now un-limited…wow…where do you start?

Start with recording short, compelling and relevant videos and posting them online. There are dozens of sites that host videos now. You can have your videos show up on ALL of these sites by going to a single site called TubeMogul. Current-ly the service is free.

You don't have to put your face on the video to get started, but it is good practice. The more practice you get with speaking publicly and on camera the easier it will be to do live inter-views on TV in the future.

First of all, broadcast television is not dead. People still tune into popular shows, news and even local television stations are readjusting to the Internet…not rolling over and dying like some newspapers.

In order to be a guest on TV, you will have to be able to "spin" your message in a timely manner. In other words, your message, on its own, probably isn't powerful enough to garner the attention of TV producers. Most of them are looking for topics that are in the news TODAY!

Is it election time? Maybe a politician is reading your book or your message is in alignment with a campaign. What about holi-days? Do you have a book about relationships? Spinning your message to Valentine's Day is easy. Keep it loose and flexible. The better you can become at adapting your message to the news, the easier it will be to contact a producer and let him/her know that you can add VALUABLE content to their broadcast.

Joint Venture

Joint venturing with people (or JV) is a sure way to build additional credibility, add to your list and increase your sales and branding. There will always be people and companies with more experience and a larger customer database than you. Seek them out and make sure you contact them in a personal and professional manner.

DO'S

- Call them on the phone. Emails will end up in the spam filter.

- Get a referral introduction from someone THEY know.

- Ask what you can do to help THEM before you ask them to help you.

DON'T

- Be a pest.

- Ask for help without giving in advance.

- Tell them anything that you can't do or haven't done.

This is where your competitors or similar businesses that are vertically integrated with you can be a tremendous lever for you. If you are a realtor in Florida, partnering with realtors in other states or a title company in FL makes good sense. If you are law-yer who has offices in 3 states, you may JV with process servers in those states. You can even JV with identical companies that don't service your area and the two of you can become stronger because of your alliance. Instead of competition you create co-opetition.

JV arrangements can leverage more than just a brand or an offer. Many high-profile companies have in-house media and media relation departments. Consider the following scenario:

A) You send out a press release announcing the publication of your book.

B) A fortune 500 company announces the publication of your book (along with a corporate purchase of 5,000 copies)

If a producer wants to report on this news, they will always go with the trusted source...the one with a household name. Before you can contact GM or Coca-Cola and ask them to part-ner with you, do your homework.

The trick is to LEVERAGE your media by aligning your-self with people and companies that have more experience, name recognition and money than you.

Your Book

 # Sell a Truckload of Books

*T*he main objective for you will be to use your book as the foundation for being recognized as the "go to" person, the expert and authority on your particular topic. As a published author, your author*ity is real, because, well…it's in print! As you start putting links to your articles, and promote your media interviews, your status rises right alongside the most recognized brands in the media. A rising tide does lift all ships and when your name is prominently displayed next to ABC, CNN, FOX, etc., it solidifies your credibility.

What would it mean if you could add a few corporate logos to your resume? What would it do for your keynote speaking, corporate training, consulting or other business if you could also add Coca Cola, Toyota, GM, Google, or Macy's to your list of alliances?

Before you think, "My book wouldn't interest a corporation," consider the following examples provided by Steve Harrison from Bradley communications in Matthew Bennett's *Sell Books By the Truckload.*

Books on all kinds of topics have been successfully sold in mass quantity. Below is a list – in no particular order – of different topic categories that have proven to be successful:

- **Health --** Does a book title like ***Lifestyles of The Trim and Healthy***, sound all that unique? I don't think so. But even though Matthew Bennett is not a medical doctor, he wrote the book, and sold 50,000 copies to a company who wanted to give it away to help sell an infomercial diet plan.

- **Christian --** One of the big reasons Rick Warren's book ***Purpose Driven Life*** has sold so many millions of copies was he focused on selling it by the truckload. Churches around the country placed large orders for the books that they then made available to their members.

- **Relationships --** Cindy Cashman has sold more than a million copies of her book ***Everything Men Know About Women***. She did it primarily by getting women's clothing stores to buy her book in mass quantity.

- **Self Help --** Did you know more than 1.1 million copies of Albert Ellis' book, ***Guide to Rational Living*** had been sold largely to groups of psychologists and self-help groups?

- **Motivational / Inspirational --** Charles "Tremendous" Jones, a well-known motivational speaker had a successful business for many years simply selling his motivational books in mass quantity to companies. They'd buy the books and give them to their salespeople in order to keep them motivated.

- **Nutrition** -- The Vitamin Shoppe did a special promotion around Jordan Rubin's *The Maker's Diet*. As an incentive to get customers to buy two bottles of vitamins instead of one, they offered a free copy of Rubin's book: buy two bottles of vitamins and get a free book!

- **Parenting** -- Matthew Bennett sold more than 3 million copies of his book *The Maternal Journal* to Ross Labs. They used it as an incentive to get people to enroll in their "Welcome Addition Club."

- **Business** -- Did you know AT&T offered free copies of a book called *Maxi Marketing* to anyone who called in to listen to their sales pitch for AT&T's solutions for direct marketers? They ran full-page ads offering the book to dozens of business magazines.

- **Photography** -- *The Colorado Scenic Calendar* ... does that sound like a book destined to sell tons of copies to companies? I don't think so. Yet Coors beer bought 100,000 copies of it to give to their distributors who then gave it as a gift to their key accounts.

- **Inspirational** -- Matthew Bennett sold 80,000 copies of his book, *In a Child's Eyes*. In fact he did it just on one phone call.

- **Memoir / Autobiography** -- *Working Woman Magazine* wanted to encourage people to subscribe so they gave copies away of *Boss Lady*, an autobiography of advertising executive Jo Foxworth.

- **Cookbooks** -- Bamberger's department store bought 50,000 copies of a cookbook titled *A Taste for German Cooking*. They used it to promote their store at Oktoberfest celebrations.

- **Careers** -- Coors Brewing Company purchased 165,000 copies of the book, *Getting Hired*, by Edward J. Rogers, and distributed them on college campuses across America as part of their continuing promotion to the youth market.

- **Travel** -- Kellogg's wanted to increase sales of Mueslix cereal. So, what did they do? They gave away copies of *Fodor's Touring Europe* with proofs of purchase. Proctor and Gamble purchased copies of *Great American Vacations* to promote – of all things – Pepto-Bismol.

- **Pets** -- Matthew Bennett sold 300,000 copies of *The Puppy Journal*. He also sold 300,000 copies of *The Kitten Journal*. And he didn't even have a pet!

- **Senior Living** -- Linda and Robert Kalian's book, *The Best Free Things for Seniors*. They've sold over 1 million copies, largely through "special sales" to companies like Publisher's Clearing House, who bought 100,000 copies of their book to use as a free giveaway.

- **Finance** -- Robert Kiyosaki, author of *Rich Dad Poor Dad*, has sold truckloads of books to MLM companies. Since his book encourages people to get into some kind of business for themselves, MLM distributors buy the book in mass quantity and make it available to people in their downline. In fact, early sales of his book in quantity to Amway was one of the keys to making his book so well known and catapulting it the *New York Times* Best Seller list where he's been for more than six years now.

- **Local Interest** -- Judy Dugan sold 5,000 copies of her self-published book, ***Santa Barbara Highlights and History***, to a bank in Santa Barbara who gave it away as part of the celebration for the opening of a new branch.

- **Gift books** -- Reader's Digest Condensed Books gave away 750,000 copies of Judith King's book, ***The Greatest Gift Guide Ever***, as a premium to sign up for their book club.

- **Technical** -- Robert Mastin of Aegis Publishing Group, publishes books on telecommunications. He's said while he may only sell 2,000 copies of a single title through bookstores, it's not uncommon for him to sell 50,000 copies of his books to a single phone company.

- **How to** -- Rita Emmett is passionate about helping people learn how to stop procrastinating. She sold more than 100,000 copies of her book in the first 14 months. She was helped by selling 8,000 copies to an Amway distributor, and another 8,000 copies to Nutrition for Life, another multi-level marketing company.

- **Sports** -- Coldwater Creek (a woman's clothing store!) placed a big order for a book titled ***The Love of Baseball***. They displayed it prominently among the women's clothing as a possible gift item women could buy for men. It was one of only two books being offered in the entire store!

- **Psychology / Mental Improvement** -- Roger Van Oech sold 2,000 copies of his self-published book, *A Whack on the Side of the Head*, to IBM to use in their training programs, and he's done this kind of bulk sales many times.

There are some distinct advantages to focusing on bulk sales after you have the momentum of your credibility campaign.

Advantage #3 – No returns. While bookstores can typically return any or all of your books for full credit, most special sales deals are done on a non-returnable basis.

Advantage #4 – Get paid up-front. Done right, with special sales you get paid BEFORE you even print the books, rather than waiting for months on end to get paid by bookstores. This means you only pay the printing bill after you sell the books.

Advantage #5 – Viral marketing. The company that buys your books endorses you to their customers and employees around the world. If you think about it, the company is paying to tell others about you, which makes this another form of viral marketing.

Advantage #6 – Raise money for charity. You can do deals to raise money for charity while you're selling books and making money. Offer to DONATE your book to a charity and use the corporation as the sponsor for the FREE book the charity receives. Offer 10,000 books to a non-profit for free. Trust me, they won't say no. Let them know in order to deliver such a sizeable gift, you'll need a corporate sponsor. Approach several corporations that would have an interest in the database of the charity. Approach them and let them know you have already struck a deal with them and are looking for a SINGLE corporate sponsor. The corporation gets to put their logo on the book (longevity) and add a cover letter to the mailing (community service). By capturing a non-profit's mission and aligning it with a corporation, you benefit three entities; the non-profit, the corporation and you. I love leverage!

The process is dissimilar to your marketing and branding strategy of appealing to the media, both social and broadcast. In those venues, you are building credibility and the status as the expert. This status reduces or eliminates your traditional marketing and "throwing mud on the wall" approach to acquiring new customers.

Your primary and initial focus is on your perception in the marketplace. Once you have established your strategy and tactics there, you can choose to move into this realm of moving a truckload of books.

The process takes time, of course, but can be well worth it after you have established yourself as the expert.

1. Create a book about a topic you are passionate about. Don't write a book about a topic simply because you think a corporation will like it. Like all sales, you will have to approach more than one prospect before you solidify a client. You can always edit the book a bit to align some of the messaging or logos to the corporate client.

2. Hire an intern or research assistant from www.guru.com or www.elance.com and have them compile a list of 100+ corporations that you feel would benefit from giving or selling your book to THEIR clients. Remember to keep your clients' client's interest in mind. The more you focus on the corporation's needs, the better.

3. Pick up the phone and call them. Too many people are depending on email or marketing to start a relationship and win customers. The old fashioned telephone is a perfect tool for making appointments. If you are not comfortable using doing this, you can hire out a professional sales person and give them a fat commission for landing you a few large clients. Post at the following sites; www.freelancer. com, www.gofreelance.com, www.craiglist.org and offer a lucrative commission. Be sure to give them some training or outline of your expectations. Don't hire desperate people. Focus on the very best you can find.

With a bit of patience and consistent effort, you can move from credible expert to best selling author in a few months. Adding that corporate logo to your site, of course, will garner more interviews and attention as well.

Chapter 11

Archimedes' Lever: Move the Earth With Your Book

Longevity of your book

Creating a book about YOU your company or brand is an exciting undertaking. It also requires a tremendous amount of thought and work. It is BECAUSE of the scope of this effort that creates the longevity, prestige and leverage you desire.

Longevity is perhaps one of the most powerful attributes at your disposal. If you compare a book against any other kind of impact or 'leave-behind' with a customer, nothing compares.

Brochures: Sure, they are glossy, impressive and tell your story. The time and money you put into creating them may be massive, but ask yourself one question, "How many brochures from YOUR vendors to you have sitting on your coffee table?" "How many times have you opened up and completely read someone else's brochure?" The longevity of a brochure (time it remains in a customer's mind) is less than 10 seconds on average. To make matters worse, sometimes your brochure isn't read at all! According to marketing maven, Seth Godin,

The thing you must remember about just about every corporate or organizational brochure is this: People won't read it.

I didn't say it wasn't important. I just said it wasn't going to get read.

People will consider its heft. They might glance at the photos. They will certainly notice the layout. And, if you're lucky, they'll read a few captions or testimonials.

At its best, a brochure is begging for someone to judge you. It says, "assume that because we could hire really good printers and photographers and designers and writers, we are talented [surgeons, real estate developers, whatever]" And more often than not, people do just that.

At its worst, a brochure solves a prospect's problem (the problem of: what should I do about this opportunity?) by giving them an easy way to say "no." "No," she thinks, "I don't need to talk with you... I've reviewed the brochure."

In short, a brochure lasts a few seconds if you are lucky. Your book, even if it's mediocre will last quite a while. People have a real aversion to throwing away books. It may have to do with our culture of freedom of the press in this country or the disgust in our stomachs when we read about groups who ban or burn books. In any event, books tend to stick around and the covers grace our bookshelves and coffee tables long after they are read.

If you book is useful, entertaining or otherwise provides good value, it can even get passed around or read more than once. That cannot be said for any other leave behind or brochure. Do you enjoy giving away post it notes and leather binders? Sure, the pen you gave away with your logo on it may stick with a client of a few months, but a book can last a lifetime…or more.

Prestige of your book

Even if your "free pen" stays on a client desk for a month or two, the prestige of a book is without challenge. Nobody looks as your business card or brochure and says, "Thanks! What a high-value thing you've given me." More likely, you, your company and your message were forgotten within moments of your gracious gift.

Value and prestige has a tremendous effect not only on the longevity of your impact on a client but also adds to the thought and care you leave behind. If your competitor sends a thank you note, he will be perceived as more caring that one who does not. When you leave your book behind, your degree of caring soars above a thank you note or Christmas card which is discarded quickly and the impact dissolves almost the very second it arrives.

If you want to double or triple your impact of your book, make it a USEFUL book for your clients. This style of book does not have to be a "how to" manual or innovative business concept. Your story, how you came into business, the challenges you faced and what you learned from your journey can provide tremendous value to your clients.

Many business owners are reluctant to share their challenges along with their success. We often shy away from our past challenges because we don't want our potential clients to see us as weak.

Nothing can be further from the truth.

You don't necessarily have to share your bankruptcy and meth addiction in your chronicles, but the more you can relate your life as a person, the more the reader will connect with you.

We do business with people we know, like and trust. Hiding the truth or avoiding important facts never establishes trust. Your clients will trust you MORE as you let them know you are a real person and NOT just a faceless corporation. We love to hear about the success of a company, but we devour books about the entrepreneur who overcame his challenges and built the company.

If your company is still in the growth phase, GREAT! Let them know.

Transparency is the new buzzword of the business world.

Be honest. Be open. Be yourself.

Stories are more interesting than facts. When you tell your story, don't embellish, but its OK to be dramatic and share your ups as much as your downs. The more interesting your book, the higher the value.

Prestige of being an author is often perceived as MORE impressive than being on the cover of a magazine. Cover stories are about a person's company or journey. A book is the telling of that journey and with YOU listed as the author, you truly are a celebrity.

Exponential Leverage

There is leverage and there is MASSIVE leverage. With the proper application of your lever (your book) and an ongoing fulcrum (media, exposure, etc.) your book cannot just be a lever, but an absolute game changer for your business.

By following a focused and consistent path of media, promotion and service, your book can land in the hand of hundreds of thousands, even millions of people. While marketing messages have the capability of doing that instantly with enough cash, only a book gives you the prestige of an expert and the longevity of being a published author.

Buying a Super bowl ad lasts 30 seconds. Newspaper, radio and even that fancy brochure of yours are amongst the thousands of other messages your prospects receive on a daily and even hourly basis. Only your book can cut through the clutter and deliver what your clients TRULY are searching for…a solution, not a sales pitch.

Sure, there are sales methods and clever "advertorials" that attempt to give your prospects the solution they want. However, anyone with a 3rd grade education knows that in the end you are trying to sell him or her something. Your book, on the other hand, is 180 degrees from that method of communication.

With your book, the prospect has ALREADY given you their money for your content. They are not being solicited AFTER they have interacted with you (You better not embed too many upsells in your book!). They have forked over their hard earned money with only one idea in their head, "Can the $20 I paid for this book entertain, inform or educate me to bring me closer to what I want?" What do they want? The same thing everyone does…love, wealth, health and happiness. If you can combine any number of these (while keeping the book consistent) all the better.

Want to have tighter abs? Read this book on how an overweight schoolteacher transformed her body and became a part time aerobics instructor! (Health combined with wealth and happiness)

The leverage of your book should take on multiple facets not only of your readers' life, but yours as well. When your book not only enhances your reputation, but also provides you a new platform for speaking, being interviewed on the radio or selling your core product, you win.

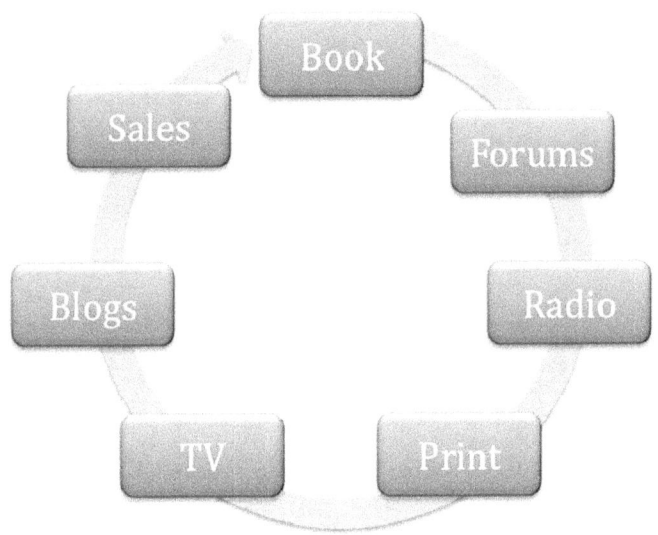

The more you expose your book in multiple media channels, the more OTHER media channels pick you up.

The more you are referenced on other websites and sources, the LESS work you have to do to promote yourself. You see, media producers are a bit lazy and it is far easier for them to NOT check you out and verify your credentials. The only way to do this is to have someone ELSE check you out! You've seen this before where a person is quoted as an expert on some topic and all of a sudden they appear on multiple TV and radio stations.

This is not just smart work on behalf of the PR person or author; it is also a natural flow from the media to trust other sources. These people are extremely busy and usually on very tight deadlines. Saving 15 minutes can be crucial.

Start with your own blog. Get published and offer your reviews, comments and opinions on as many other RESPECTED sites as you can.

Drop us a line and we can send you a FREE guide to help you be interviewed by top radio personalities as often as you wish. The more you link to THEIR station sites and interact with them, the more you become an insider.

Giving Your Book Away

Huh? You just invested 8 months of your life, $25,000 in proofing, graphics, layout, design and expenses and you want to give away your heart, soul and your child for FREE? Are you crazy?

That depends.

Giving away ALL of your book in EVERY available format does cheapen the message and dilutes the value. I would not recommend giving away a printed copy for free to anyone without any quid pro quo. Many people give away samples or bundle their book with OTHER offerings as a way to add value.

Strangely, digital downloads of many books used to be HIGHER than printed versions, even though this format is virtually free for the publisher. With the proliferation of digital books (read on the Kindle, iPad, etc.) "publishing" has transformed forever. Giving away a chapter or two has never been easier.

Be sure, of course, to capture the prospects contact information in exchange for these chapters. You'll want to measure the results of campaigns like that to test, measure and improve the effectiveness. Marketing is never static and your constant measurement and improvement of it, is vital.

How well does your marketing perform?

If you are good, really good at developing and expanding the pain of the problem your book solves for the reader, you can charge more. This is true in fiction and non-fiction alike.

The hardback copy of the last Harry Potter book will likely be more expensive than the soft cover version a year or so later. Why? It has the same content. The words don't change? What about the movie? You will be able to see a full (probably 3D) version of the book for around $10! And that movie cost WAY more to produce than the book. In fact, if you wait a year or so, you can see that EXACT same movie for $1 by renting it from Redbox!

Your book has value.

It can be permissible and even encouraged to give part or all of your book away for free providing you abide by some or all of the criteria below:

1. Give away a portion as a "sample" as to the value of the rest of the book.

2. Give away the book in full as a "bonus" to your other products or service.

3. Give it away because there are compelling links to other products inside.

4. Give away a small number of copies to encourage others to buy.

5. Give away a small number of copies as part of a sales contest or promotion.

6. Give away the book as a pdf instantly while waiting for shipment of the book.

7. Give away the book as a course manual.

Making Money ON your book

Of course, the idea of selling a million copies and receiving a $1 for every copy would make you a millionaire. There are hundreds of stories of how a book made authors and "overnight" success. Mark Victor Hansen and Jack Canfield (and hundreds of others) used their first book to launch a series. By creating a framework that you can duplicate, you not only insure the longevity of your brand, you can create additional income streams as an ongoing profit center. Below are more examples:

Guerilla Marketing

Automatic Millionaire

Chicken Soup for the Soul

Harry Potter

Or even brands like…

John Grisham

Steven King

Clive Cussler

Upsells, Teasers and Raving Fans

Your book can be the most powerful sales brochure in existence. So often, business owners try to use clever copy, compelling sales arguments, incentives and "freebies" in order to capture the loyalty of their clients.

It is always best to use your OWN experience as a guide. When you last made a significant purchase, reflect on your thought process. Did you get a referral? Did you take a test drive? Did the reputation of the company seal the deal?

Would you more likely take financial advice from a company with a slick and compelling sales campaign or from a known author who you saw in the media?

When you use your book as the foundation for your message, you not only elevate your status, but you can continue to educate, inform and sell to your fans additional products or services.

It's an upsell if a fast food place asks you if you want dessert after you meal.

It's a brilliant marketer that describes the award winning ice-cream creation BEFORE the meal!

Deliver good content above all else. When you do that, so long as you continue to deliver value, you can continue to turn a one-time customer into a long-term client and raving fan.

List 5 ways your book can leverage your brand, image and company

1. _____

2. _____

3. _____

4. _____

5. _____

Chapter 12

$10K/day Author: Speaking, Coaching & Licensing

*D*reaming, fantasizing and wishing can be extremely productive motivators if the nature of your internal voice is positive, rewarding and empowering. As an entrepreneur you may need to guard against wasting huge amounts of time daydreaming in a free-floating manner without focusing your mind on the specific dreams you would like to achieve.

If you are already a speaker earning $10,000, $20,000 or more for a keynote talk, you already have a book and probably aren't even reading this! The reason I mention that is because professional speakers are keenly aware of the value of a book and have established themselves as a valuable expert that can command 5 figure speaking gigs BECAUSE they are a published author, maybe even a best selling author.

In order to earn $10,000, $20,000 or more from an hour or two of work you consider the following:

1. **Value.** Your value as an expert is higher when you are a published author. There are plenty of business consultants who charge big fat fees who are not authors, but the ones who are, especially best sellers have a tremendous advantage. In addition to charging more per hour than their non-author competitors, a published author is better suited to execute virtual training, teleseminars and market other high margin intellectual property.

2. **Speaking**. There are countless areas where you can become a highly sought after and well-compensated speaker. Check the resource section of this book to see a list of books, training programs and associations that can accelerate and build your speaking career. Suffice to say, I learned my lesson as a speaker years ago that without a book, I was not only short changing my revenue stream by not having a modestly priced item for attendees (many speaker focus only on pitching high-priced products) but I was missing out on the more important concept of building a loyal following. In any given crowd, there are always going to be more people who are not ready to buy from you right now vs. those who are. However, the operative word is *now*… by having a $20 book available for anyone (include tax with that price…most people carry a $20 bill in their wallet) you are drawing a larger crowd into your fan base than if you simply leave them a brochure. If 200 people attend your talk and 30 of them become clients of your high priced

product, you are effectively blowing through 170 qualified leads! Translate that to the online world. If you could capture someone's attention for an hour online, don't you think you have a huge chance of at least capturing their contact information, if not their hearts and minds?

Having a quality book should allow a decent speaker to capture at least half of the room for later. If you are worried that people will opt for the book in lieu of your high-priced product, my suggestion is to add some training to your speaking and "closing from the platform" education. There is no reason you can't address the budgets of an entire audience without sacrificing sales of your high end products.

3. **Training**. Many speakers use their book, keynote speaking and other intellectual property in order to sell corporate or group training. Training organizations allows you to duplicate your efforts and move from one-on-one coaching to group training-effectively increasing your per hour rate. Why coach one person at $100 per hour when you can train a group of 10 for $25/each? Authors always command larger fees for speaking and training. Your celebrity status dictates a higher level of authority and resultant value in the minds of your clients.

4. **Licensing**. After you become an author and the momentum of your brand is strong, consider licensing your intellectual property. It is possible to license your method, system or brand, but to attempt to do so without a published book begs the question, "Why do you feel your material is license-worthy?" Licensing provides massive potential for

royalty based income and can eclipse any professional practice 100 fold. Examples include Stephen Covey's Franklin Day Planner and "7 Habits for Highly Effective People" John Gray's "Men are from Mars, Women are from Venus" Bob Burg's "Endless Referrals" and even the rock band KISS has licensed everything from beach towels to coffins. All of these multi-millionaires earn massive, royalty-based income from the creation of intellectual property. Every single one has at least one book...most have a series.

Mark Victor Hansen and Jack Canfield started with a single book, "Chicken Soup for the Soul." It was a clever idea that was rejected by hundreds of publishers. The publisher who finally gave them the thumbs up was down on his luck and close to going out of business. Once their first book took off, they drilled down into well over 100 hundred niches such as "Chicken Soup for the Pet Lover's Soul," "Chicken Soup for the Nurse's Soul," and "Chicken Soup for the Teen's Soul." To name a few.

Consider the massive book series "XYZ For Dummies!" I continue to be amazed at the incredible amount of niches that single title has generated for the creators of that series.

Realize that I said "creators" not authors. The owners of that brand certainly don't write every single book. To date, there are over 1,700 individual titles from the original "DOS for dummies" to one I recently saw my daughter carrying, "Opera for Dummies."

What can your brand, company, idea or intellectual property create? Don't think in terms of a single book for you and your company. Think big. Act big. Even if you achieve only 1% of the success of these media moguls, you can rest assured that your royalty income will grow and continue for decades to come.

Your book is critical to your success as an expert. But your largest and most stable income will not come from treating patients, drafting legal documents or managing a franchise. With the right concept and a consistent intellectual property creation, intelligently positioned, your financial and time freedom will come from your book and the dozens of royalty-based profit centers available to authors including speaking, coaching, training, licensing, franchising, etc.

NOTE: 99% of the people will NEVER take the time to create and publish their book.
Go DIRECTLY to the last chapter and learn about our system where we DO IT ALL for you.
www.authoryourbrand.com

Chapter 13

We Do it ALL For You

*L*et's face it; the "experts" who get the publicity, fame, credibility and major media exposure are the professionals who've published their book.

With tens of thousands of competitors in your field, the top 5% have a book that exponentially increase their following and presence in the marketplace. The top 1% has a best-selling book, a public profile, recognizable brand and bankable value. Being an author can catapult your enterprise and reputation onto a national and international platform that will outlast your lifetime.

Strategically creating high influence and a broad reach requires not only a book, but also a sophisticated marketing, focused promotion and seamless distribution plan.

Like most professionals, however, you're busy. You've no doubt thought dozens of times, "I should write a book." If only you had the capacity and the time to manage such a large-scale undertaking.

You know a book would elevate your business and your brand to rock-star status. But the reality entails…

- Many months or years from start to finish.

- Endless hours of painstaking writing, revisions and proofing.

- Finding and collaborating with an editor for months after the initial writing is completed.

- Attracting a quality-publishing agent who's properly connected in the right space.

- Managing a dedicated team to deliver your design, layout, proof and PR.

- Securing a publishing deal with a significant publisher.

- Hiring a team to promote a national and international marketing campaign.

- Hiring freelancer or staff to support all those moving parts and unknown variables.

- Allocating several hours every day for months on end, even after your book is published.

It is often difficult to visualize being an author. Even if you realize the hurdles of creation, you may be suffering from two opposing ends of the creation/idea specturm:

1. The idea that their ideas aren't unique enough or compelling enough for a book. Their business is a commodity and there isn't a clever or interesting manner to position their products or services.

2. The concept of their "life story" is so unique that it should be a movie. Their journey has significance and needs to be told to the entire world! It's a guaranteed best seller.

In either case (negative or positive) you will benefit from an honest, third-party conversation with us. Our team of journalists, writers, editors and movie producers knows the landscape and the competition. We can tell you honestly if your idea has merit or not.

Moreover, within a few minutes, we generally can take your USP, industry or brand and leverage it with the dozens of other clients we are serving. You may have a joint venture deal done BEFORE you ever start your book!

What if there was a smart alternative?

What if you could share your unique life story, philosophy and success strategies through a book that:

- Is compelling, unique and highly marketable.

- Gets you and your message out to the world effectively.

- Is written, published and market-ready in about 90 days.

- Has a built-in publishing deal from the start.

- Will be distributed on www.amazon.com and dozens of other sites.

- Is made available digitally on Kindle and iPad.

What will the above exposure and activity do for you AND your business?

Using proprietary Bexsi™ technology and the personalized human interaction from us, YOUR book and a personalized marketing machine can be up and running in just a few weeks.

Without disrupting your schedule or investing huge amounts of time, you will overwhelm your co mpetition with your new celebrity status as an author. Your book will provide you with the notoriety you deserve elevating your brand and position light years ahead of your industry competitors. You'll have authored your very own book (Hardback, soft cover, Kindle and iPad) with ease, speed and economy.

Your celebrity status as an author is not only guaranteed, but your physical soft or hard cover book will be delivered to you in less time than you think. Packages include:

Your Book

Unique 150-200 page hardcover book about you delivered in 100 days!

- Your name appears as the author (By...)

- Your picture on the cover

- Your 'bio' and photo appear on the back jacket (About...)

- Your core message customized to you and your industry

Options

Client Action Guide & Journal: Upsells and Membership Revenue

- Personalized "action guide" empowers your clients & prospects

- Customized "goal journal" keeps your message in front of your clients

- Automated "client interaction" cements client engagement with you

TV, Radio and Web Publicity package

- In-demand PR, including national radio exposure

- Guaranteed Amazon "Best Seller" status

- Virtual book tour

The Process

Your commitment of time to this project is measured in hours, not years and includes completing a tailored questionnaire, scheduling an interview with our staff and furnishing a handful of high-quality digital images. Our team takes over from there, quickly delivering a polished and published professional book, authored by YOU! You'll receive 50 copies of your book that you can proudly display, distribute or sell. You'll always have the option of buying additional copies of your book, whether for sale, to be given away or used as high-impact branding tools that highlight YOU as the expert in your field. (e.g. for journalists and other media outlets, speaking presentations and beyond)

For more information and a private consultation to see if you qualify contact us at 800-708-2757 or doug@dougcrowe. com.

Is this expensive?

That depends…

Becoming a published author will make a massive difference in your business and posistioning provided you get your book into the hands of your prospcts. For many people, increasing their business by 5, 10 or 20% can mean tens of thousands of dollars in incremental revenue. When you calcualte the lifetime value of a client, these numbers are actually much higher.

Many business owners look at their clients and the revenue in a transactional manner. Client pays "A" and that's that. But the lifetime value of a client means you develop a relationship with that person and they buy from you over and over again. You serve them well by underpromising and overdelivering and they refer a few people who also buy your products and services for years.

What does this number represent for your business?

If you are a car repair facility, the lifetime value of a client is well over $10,000. It doesn't matter if you are a personal trainer, flower shop owner or a doctor, your knowledge can be packaged in the form of CD's or DVD's (downloads nowadays), seminars, bootcamps, coaching or workshops. Your book is only the tip of the iceberg of selling your unique method, style, story and solution to your clients.

In fact, even if your business is as simple as applying makeup, you can easily pick up a private label line of brushes and cosmetics that you can sell to your followers.

The list is endless.

Therefore, the VALUE of being a published author can easily exceed $100,000, $500,000 or more.

But that incremental revenue won't come in unless you are the published expert. Writing the book comes first and creating your book costs money.

Below are a few creative ideas to raise the capital necessary to fund the creation of your book.

How to raise the money you need to write, edit and publish your book

It doesn't matter if you write your book yourself or hire a ghost writer, the dozens of people and resources necessary to craft a compelling story, publish it and create awareness of your book requires capital.

You need money to publish a book.

In rare cases, your story may be so compelling that a publisher will pay you an advance for your work. This is about as likely as winning the lottery. It happens, but unless you are a current, best-selling author, most publishing companies don't take the risk of working with new authors.

Moreover, traditional publishing companies do very little to market your book for you. They have great distribution channels, but prefer to work with authors with an existing platform and loyal following.

Self-publishing has evolved into not only a necessary option, but to those with the perseverance to do all that is necessary-a potentially lucrative one.

If you have the skill to write well and,

If you have the patience to build a platform and,

If you have the capital to hire team members.

Even if you are a good writer, nobody has the time (or skill) to do ALL the following tasks to get your book out into the world. As a writer, at the very least you will need help in the following areas:

- **Editor.** Someone to view your work objectively and help create better flow.

- **Proofer.** Someone to catch the mistakes spell & grammar check will miss.

- **Layout.** Someone to break up the manuscript and make it easy to read.

- **Format.** Convert your work to PDF, Kindle, iPad & Nook.

- **Designer.** People judge a book by its cover. Yours must be great.

- **Marketing.** Joint ventures, sponsorships. The list is endless.

- **Social Media.** Engage with your readers.

- **Media.** Get your book reviewed by newspapers, radio and TV.

- **ISBN & copyright.** Categorizing and tracking your work.

- **Distribution.** How do you get your book into multiple channels?

The list is endless, but your bank account isn't. To get started in crafting your book or even establishing a launch and campaign program to create awareness, you'll need money. Here are a few ideas to create your own "publisher's advance."

Pre-Sales

Everyone has a list of people that know them. You may be one of those reclusive writers without a huge network of influence, but when you start writing down who you know and who knows you, you'll have a list of friends, family, business contacts and neighbors.

Make a list.

Your database is your initial seed to selling the first few copies of your book. Many people will want to give away copies to friends and family. While this is pretty common, don't give away too many. People don't value as much a free book as one they pay $15 or $20 for. When appropriate, get them to buy it.

A 'pre-sale' is when you establish your theme, message and BENEFIT to your target audience. Through a blog, email or other notification, you can ask your list to pre-order your book well in advance of publishing. With a strong following of 500, 1,000 or more people and a reasonable incentive to 'pre-order' some authors can fund a significant amount of the capital required to create and publish their book.

Risks

If you do take deposits and/or pre-sales on your book, you are entering into an agreement. An agreement that involves the exchange of money. In other words, you MUST finish and DELIVER your book. There needs to be a deadline and you must meet this deadline or finish early.

No exceptions.

If you are delayed or don't finish your book, you'll be in trouble. You've taken money and not delivered an item. Refunding that money won't be as painful as explaining why you can't deliver what your promised. This method is not for the faint of heart. Finish what you start. Put the deposits in escrow and DON'T TOUCH IT!

Sell 10 Books to each person

When Bill Glazer (from Glazer-Kennedy) launched his book, *Outrageous Advertising that's Outrageously Successful*, he didn't simply pre-sell the books one at a time. He multplied his marketing, exposure and sales by a factor of ten. Here is what he did.

1. He set up an education campaign to his list. This campaign gave video testimonials and plenty of social proof to the effectiveness of the book. He gave you solid reasons why others have benefited from his message.

2. He offered a FREE electronic version of the book BEFORE the physical copy would be shipped. Charter members would get a sneak preview!

3. He offered a $1,000 FREE ticket to his seminar if you bought 10 copies (keep one and give 9 away as gifts).

Give away more value than you ask for in compensation. Make it real. Deliver.

Investors

One client of mine wisely developed more than just a book. His fitness business was local but his unique message was international. He knew that in order to grow beyond his brick and mortar gym he would have to create products and services that could be distributed regionally, nationally and even internationally. He designed the expansion of his enterprise via an education-based marketing format.

- His first order of business was to create a controversial (to get more media attention), high-quality book. With this book, he could become recognized as a credible expert in his field.

- He also established a line of supplements that his trainers would sell and that could also be marketed online. These were private-label, generic supplements that anyone could sell. He would simply put his name on them.

- He also created a membership site where people could get feedback on their training, get virtual coaching (group and private) via the internet and videos. These trainings were designed uniquely for his methodology and system. They were delivered digitally and in physical formats.

With this trilogy of education, products and services he went to a group of investors who believed in him.

Because he had a compelling message and a PLAN to expand his enterprise they listened.

Because he generously offered a stake in the business, they invested their money.

It doesn't matter what type of book you want to write, people are hungry for relevant and effective solutions to their problems. There are tens of thousands of self-development books that all have pretty much the same message. It is the unique spin and positioning an author places on that book that makes it unique.

The positioning and marketing of your message makes all the difference in the world. When you position your message in a unique (and sometimes controversial manner) you will attract attention…not only of your readers, but investors as well.

Joint Venture

Your unique message or story may change or even save the lives of thousands of people. If you don't believe that, then don't bother writing. Changing or improving lives is a common theme of most books.

Even if your book is a novel, the entertainment value of a book can affect the winds of change, bolster a movement or help a non-profit raise millions. I know of a science fiction writer who is working with a mobile game developer to create a game based on his book. They stand to reap the massive rewards of both markets.

There are dozens of variations on the sponsorship/joint venture/non-profit model. Here is one that has worked for many authors and can work for virtually any book imaginable.

Your Book

Your book has a central theme and specific benefit to a reader. It may make them happier, wealthier, wiser or simply feel better. Your book can easily be aligned with the mission statmement of any number of non-profit organizations. For example:

How to avoid Foreclosure could be helpful to members of any group dealing with finances, poverty, social services.

Eliminating Obesity could be useful for the American Heart Association or any organization dealing with health issues.

Responsiblity: Teen Guide to Becoming an Adult could be a great book for any organization that deals with youth dealing with self-esteem issues or addiction.

Step-by-step

1. Approach a non-profit that has a relevant message and mission that is in alighment with the core principles in your book.

2. Offer to give them FREE copies to their top 100,000 constituents. (They will say, "Yes!") Remind them that the value of giving a book is timeless. People may or may not use calendars. People may or may not use their cute holiday cards. A pebook lasts forever. Nobody discards a book. A book has value. A book from them says they value their constituents.

3. Let them know that in order to fund this free book, you will approach a few corporations that are in alignment with the non-profit's mission. This corporation will sponsor the purchase and shipping of this gift in exchange for a cover letter and possibly an endorsement on the book's dust jacket.

4. You approach the corporation and ask them if they would like to particiapte in a direct SOLO mailing to the top 100,000 constituents of non-profit XYZ. Remind them they

have similar values and that this "mailing" consists of a book, not some trinket or sales copy that is discarded 99% of the time. They will be getting massive non-advertising exposure and goodwill with people they want to reach.

5. Let them know that your book can be purchased at a steep discount and that you have already negotiated to put the corporation's logo on the book and include an impactful cover letter with each mailing reminding the recipient of the corporation's alignment with the non-profit.

With this system, you can actually move tens of thousands (if not hundreds of thousands) of books with a single transaction. Your focus on serving the needs of both entities is what makes this type of deal happen.

You should discount the book, but you can also include a nominal 10-20% management fee to set-up and manage the entire process. There are dozens of ways to create the capital you need to create, publish and market your book. These are thee ways you can start the process BEFORE your book is even done.

Good luck!

NOTE: 99% of the people will NEVER take the time to create and publish their book.
Go DIRECTLY to our website and learn about our system where we DO IT ALL for you.
www.authoryourbrand.com

~~Conclusion~~ Beginning

You have a book inside you. Actually, you have a book series inside you. I believe you have a tremendous, marketable brand within the walls of your mind. Unleash your ideas, put them in print and serve your clients, partners and even your competition by being what Bob Burg calls, a "Go-Giver." By giving and serving selflessly, you will garner more fans and clients than simply marketing.

By dedicating yourself to completing your book, marketing yourself and your brand, you have taken the most difficult step towards separating yourself from your competition and solidifying your enterprise.

Refer to the chapters you have read often. Writers always need a kick in the pants, a seed of inspiration and a team to pull off this massive yet completely satisfying task of creating a book.

Our company is available to assist you in any way you need. Don't hesitate to drop us a line or ask us a question. We are here to serve in any way you need.

~Doug Crowe
www.dougcrowe.com
www.authoryourbrand.com
doug@dougcrowe.com
800-708-2757

 # Resources

PUBLISHING COMPANIES

www.authorhouse.com

www.publishing.morgan-james.com

BOOK PRINTING

www.lulu.com

www.48hrbooks.com

www.instantpublisher.com

www.cafepress.com

www.createspace.com

www.lightningsource.com

TRANSCRIPTION SERVICES

www.transcriptionstar.com

www.elance.com

www.guru.com

ARTICLE DIRECTORIES

www.ezinearticles.com

www.articlesbase.com

AFFILIATE SITES

www.amazon.com

www.clickbank.com

www.commissionjunction.com

www.indiebound.com

www.paydotcom.com

www.payloadz.com

ISBN & BAR CODES

RR Bowker

630 Central Avenue, New Providence, NJ 07974 Tel: 888-269-5372 E-mail: info@bowker.com http://www.bowker.com

FineLine Technologies

Richard Jaynes "Serving the publishing industry for more than 15 years! Fastest service, competitive pricing! Preferred provider to Amazon.com! " 157 Technology Parkway, #700, Norcross, GA 30092 Tel: 800-500-8687; Fax: 678-969-9201

E-mail: orders@FineLineTech.com http://www.FineLineTech.com

AccuGraphiX

Tracy Warman "Quality electronic files, film masters or labels. Referred/approved by ISBN/Bowker, the Uniform Code Council and Amazon.com." 3588 East Enterprise Drive, Anaheim, CA 92807-1627 Tel: 800-872-9977; Fax: 714-630-6581 E-mail: agxaztek@earthlink.net http://www.bar-code.com

Film Masters

Kathy Paugh "Fast, courteous service for film masters, electronic files and labels." 11680 Hawke Road, Columbia Station, OH 44028 Tel: 800-541-5102; Fax: 800-826-1410 E-mail: BarCodes@en.com http://www.FilmMasters.com

Fotel, Inc.

"Film masters, EPS files & bar code labels and any other labels. " 1125 E St. Charles Rd., Suite 100; Lombard, IL 60148 Tel: 800-834-4920; Fax: 630-932-7610 E-mail: sales@fotel. com

http://www.fotel.com

SOCIAL NETWORKING SITES

www.facebook.com

www.twitter.com

www.plus.google.com

www.linkedin.com

www.youtube.com

www.tubemogul.com

www.growl.com

www.delicious.com

www.digg.com

www.diigo.com

www.gather.com

www.mixx.com

www.newsvine.com

www.reddit.com

www.stumbleupon.com

CONSULTANTS

Doug Crowe:

Author, speaker and facilitator for entrepreneurs, professionals and business owners. Provides the only "Single Point of Contact" to create, develop, write, publish and produce a completed book for professionals and entrepreneurs. www.dougcrowe. com www.authoryourbrand.com

Bexsi, www.bexsi.com is the company's proprietary interactive accountability book that mirrors a person's personality and creates a physical book and "Nag-O-Matic" accountability system that delivers a speakers book, message and experiential learning system after a book is completed.

Rich Frishman:

AUTHOR101 UNIVERSITY Live event in Las Vegas, New York and Los Angeles. 3 times a year. 15 speakers, editors, literary agents and marketing experts. For all entrepreneurs, and want to be authors. In a phrase, Rick is one of the good guys.

His experience is second only to his giving spirit and sincere love for the game.

www.author101university.com

Dan Poynter:

Author (100+ books), publisher (since 1969) and speaker (CSP). His seminars have been featured on CNN, his books have been pictured in The Wall Street Journal and his story has been told in US News & World Report. Dan is a past vice-president of the Publishers Marketing Association. www.parapublishing.com

Tom Antion:

Tom has taught thousands of people how to make money as a speaker. You will find moneymaking tips and techniques savvy speakers use to make money with their mouth and mind. www.amazingpublicspeaking.com

ASSOCIATIONS

Local PRSA Chapters

www.prsa.org

The Institute for PR

www.instituteforpr.com

American Society of Association Executives

www.asaenet.org

International Association of
Business Communicators

www.iabc.com

National Investor Relations Institute NIRI)

www.niri.org

American Marketing Association

www.ama.org

Business Marketing Association

www.marketing.org

National Speakers Association

The premier association for experts who speak professionally.

http://www.nsaspeaker.org

ABA

Bookweb, the American Booksellers Association site. Guide to
Media Marketing http://www.ambook.org

BOOK FULFILLMENT SERVICES

CCI (Headquarters)

They print softcover, hardcover, spiral bound and just about anything you want. CCI is a mid-size company with a small town feel. I love these guys. 1225 Walnut Ridge Drive

Hartland, WI 53029 Toll Free: 1-800-332-2348 Tel: 262-369-6000 Fax: 262-369-5647 email: Tim.Enright@comcom.com http://www.comcom.com/

Alexander's Digital Printing

Barry Merrell "High quality experienced POD digital printing. We understand publishers' needs." 245 South 1060 West, Lindon, UT 84042-1606 Tel: 800-574-8666; Fax: 801-224-0446 E-mail: BarryM@Alexanders.com http://www.Alexanders.com

Book Clearing House (BCH)

Nancy Smoller "Book Order Fulfillment. One percentage charge covers everything." 46 Purdy Street, Harrison, NY 10528 Tel: 800-431-1579; Fax: 914-835-0398 E-mail: BookCH@aol.com http://www.BookCH.com

BookMasters, Inc.

Cathy Purdy "Complete one-stop book manufacturing source. Composition/ Printing/ Binding/Fulfillment/Web sales/E-Publishing." 2541 Ashland Road, Mansfield, OH 44905 Tel: 800-537-6727; Fax: 419-589-4040

E-mail: info@BookMasters.com http://www.BookMasters.com

PSI Fulfillment

Ben Sorrell "Warehousing; order-taking online + 800# call center); credit cards; shipping." 8803 Tara Lane, Austin, TX 78737 Tel: 800-460-0500; Fax: 512-288-5055 E-mail: ben@psiFulfillment.com http://www.psiFulfillment.com

For more links, resources and potential team members, contact us at doug@dougcrowe.com or go to www.authoryourbrand.com and register for our free newsletter. We also have online, highly interactive classes to teach you not only the nuts and bolts, but a dedicated team to do everything for you, if that is your choice.

www.ingramcontent.com/pod-product-compliance
Lightning Source LLC
Chambersburg PA
CBHW051506170526
45166CB00001B/415